TO DWELL WITH FELLOW CLAY

The Story of
East Cleveland Township Cemetery

BY
NANCY FOGEL WEST

Bloomington, IN Milton Keynes, UK

authorHOUSE™

AuthorHouse™
1663 Liberty Drive, Suite 200
Bloomington, IN 47403
www.authorhouse.com
Phone: 1-800-839-8640

AuthorHouse™ UK Ltd.
500 Avebury Boulevard
Central Milton Keynes, MK9 2BE
www.authorhouse.co.uk
Phone: 08001974150

First published by AuthorHouse 5/10/2007

ISBN: 978-1-4259-8695-7 (sc)

Library of Congress Control Number: 2007901387

Printed in the United States of America
Bloomington, Indiana

This book is printed on acid-free paper.

Contents

Introduction

Over the past several years many people have asked how I became interested in the East Cleveland Township Cemetery. The answer to that question is simple. A search for the history of my father's family (Richard F. Fogel (1923-1996)) began after his death in January, 1996. I had lost my sister (Deborah Ann Fogel (1959-1993)) in July, 1993 and now my father was gone. The family was dwindling and I had never known my Grandfather Reuben Fogel as he had passed away prior to my parent's marriage and my Grandmother Wanda (nee May) Fogel never said much about the family. The search began with trying to find out more about my grandfather, Reuben Fogel. His obituary revealed that he had brothers and sisters who we had never met. After several years of research and putting the Fogel family tree together through obituaries, death certificates, United States census records, and Swedish church records, I had accounted for several hundred family members in the Cleveland area most of who were now deceased. The only way to connect with these ancestors was to visit their graves. The names of the cemeteries where they were buried were obtained from their death certificates. Trips were made to Lake View Cemetery, Woodland Cemetery, Scranton Road Cemetery and in August 1999, my mother Arlene (nee Gutzman) Fogel, cousin Judy (nee Kalnofske) Evridge and myself made our maiden journey from Medina County to East Cleveland Township Cemetery. The goal was to find the graves of my great-grandfather's brothers, Gustav and Carl Fogel. Upon arriving we had no idea where these brothers and their wives were buried; we spread out in different directions and just started walking the cemetery reading headstones and were fortunate to find them within a couple hours.

The East Cleveland Township Cemetery became imbedded in my visual memory because of its mature beauty and peacefulness; the cemetery itself was also being forgotten and its records were difficult to access. In July, 2002 I traveled to Sweden where my Fogel ancestors were from and found it amazing to see the lengths small communities, as well as the country as a whole, took to preserve their heritage. Initially, it was very clear that something needed to be done to help others find their ancestors in the East Cleveland Township Cemetery. A project was born. With the approval and encouragement of the Service Department in the City of East Cleveland, I went to the Service Department every other Tuesday evening after work for over a year and scanned each of the burial index cards. From these scanned images I manually input the information into a database and ultimately placed the information on the internet to ease others search for their ancestors (www.rootsweb. com/~ohcuycem). As I typed all the names, dates and causes of death into the database I started to wonder just who these people were who died so long ago.

There was also the question about the history of the cemetery itself as to how it got started, was there a church somewhere that it was associated with, and why was it being neglected and forgotten. It was decided that this little cemetery (approximately 12 acres) having been forgotten by most and unknown to most Clevelanders had to have a story to tell, as did the over 17,000 people who were laid to rest within its gates. Perhaps part of the reason most Clevelanders have no knowledge of the cemetery is due to the fact that is surrounded by residential housing and the railroad. As the search began there were many urban legends found regarding the cemetery. The research has been difficult because fact had to be separated from fiction. Records regarding the cemetery were also difficult to locate and there was no previous research regarding the cemetery.

The journey of researching the history of East Cleveland Township Cemetery could not have been accomplished without the assistance of many people who were patient when I kept asking questions trying to find the truth, namely, the staff at the Cuyahoga County Recorders Office, Western Reserve Historical Society, Cuyahoga County Archives, and Cuyahoga County Common Pleas Court. Kris Tapei Fay, a graphic designer and one of East Cleveland Township Cemetery's volunteers who designed the East Cleveland Township Cemetery Foundation's logo, letterhead and brochures, assisted with the name of the book and the graphic design of the cover. J. Wayne Rhine provided the photographs of the cemetery that is on the book's cover. There are also all the friends, family members and co-workers who listened to my incessant talking about the cemetery. However, one person stands out in the crowd and is the reason that I finally took the leap to attempt to write this history and that is Walter C. Leedy, Jr. I am not a historian by trade and have never attempted such a task as this; without Walter's coaching and nudging I may never have had the courage to take this ultimate step. Unfortunately Walter passed away prior to this story being published, but he was able to read and provide invaluable guidance and suggestions.

The title of this book "To Dwell with Fellow Clay" is taken from one of the cemetery's older headstones and was placed in memory of Smith Towner. Mr. Towner was a farmer in Independence and passed away on August 11, 1833. He was one of many people who were later transferred into East Cleveland Township Cemetery from what is now referred to as the former Doan's Corner Cemetery. The verse carved on the marker reads as follows:

> *Great God I own my sentence just*
> *And nature must decay*
> *I yield my body to the dust*
> *To dwell with fellow clay*
> *As you are now so once was I*
> *Prepare for death for you must die.*

The first four lines of the verse were actually taken from Isaac Watt's (1674-1748) hymn "Triumph over Death". Mr. Watts also is credited with writing the hymn "Joy to the World"

What is clear is that in the late 1800's and early 1900's there were two cemeteries referred to as East Cleveland Cemetery. The first and oldest was originally called the "Publick Burying Ground" when it was established in 1823. In later years the Publick Burying Ground was called the Doan's Corner Cemetery, the old East Cleveland Cemetery and the little cemetery on Euclid Avenue. By the early 1900's the Publick Burying Ground was closed and the bodies re-interred elsewhere. The East Cleveland Township Cemetery that still exists today was established in 1859 and was also referred to as the East Cleveland Cemetery and for several years as the East Cleveland-Cleveland Heights Cemetery. The stories of both cemeteries will be told as you can not tell one without the other.

Before beginning we need to remember that we are looking at these cemeteries in the early to mid 1800's. By the mid-1800's when the East Cleveland Township Cemetery was established the Township of East Cleveland extended from what is now East 55th Street (formerly Willson Avenue) east out Euclid Avenue to Windermere. Doan's Corner was part of the Township of East Cleveland and was located around what is now the intersection of East 105th and Euclid Avenue. During this time period some referred to Doan's Corner as "the second downtown". The area where East Cleveland Township Cemetery is located has been part of the City of Cleveland since 1892.

The story of East Cleveland Township Cemetery is directed to those individuals who are interested in the history of our grand City of Cleveland both from a historical as well as a genealogical perspective. We need to honor, cherish and hold close to our hearts the trials and tribulations of all our ancestors and what they did over 200 years ago so that we could have what we have today. The story of the East Cleveland Township Cemetery is written with the hope that our history and heritage will not be lost and will be revitalized through the telling of its story.

At this point you may be asking yourself, why should we care what happens to this little tract of cemetery land and its permanent residents. In the *Cleveland Plain Dealer* on July, 3, 1988, Brent Larkin put forth the following commentary regarding the cemetery and why we should care and remember:

Tomorrow is for our forefathers.

It's for the gallant men and women who made this country possible, for those pioneers who endured the tough times in the late 18th century, enabling us to celebrate good times in the late 20th century.

It's tough to imagine what life was like around these parts 212 years ago, but some things we do know.

While the likes of Washington and Jefferson were engineering a nation's freedom in the east, men named Hiram Day, Frederick Silsby, Dr. Elijah Burton, Stephen B. Meeker and Hugh Davy were helping shape Cleveland's future in the Midwest.

I don't know much about this particular group of early Clevelanders, except that they were all born a couple centuries ago and their remains now rest within a few feet of one another.

These men and women are prisoners in one of the most despicable, unkempt, revolting, filthy places imaginable. They have the grave misfortune of being buried in the East Cleveland-Cleveland Heights Cemetery, a 12-acre tract of shame tucked off a sidestreet on Cleveland's far East Side.

Very few Clevelanders probably do not even know this ancient cemetery exists. The small, heavily wooded burial ground is on E. 118th St. not far from Euclid Ave. and only a stone's throw from the scenic Lake View Cemetery.[1]

The 1916 President of the Early Settlers Association, Alexander Hadden, described those individuals that this story is directed:

In a rough sort of way, folks can be divided into three classes. There is a class of people who are always looking into the future. If they could have their way they would travel ahead of the sun and live in a constant dawn; they love to see dark places light up. They love to see new things; they feed on newness. The second class are those who live in that very short space of time called the present. They are like children on a railroad train. They don't care, where they came from; they don't care where they are going, but they like to look out the window and see what they are surrounded by. Then there is the third class who, if they could have their way, would travel backward, with their back to the sun and live in a perpetual twilight; the landscape would always be fading and glimmering; their interest is in what has gone before. They love to trace back the present to the past.[2]

So as you read this story, look into the future and visualize what your children or grandchildren might learn from the early struggles that made this great City; or live in the present and enjoy the natural beauty that is now East Cleveland Township Cemetery; or if you are really courageous step back in time and try to understand and experience the lives of our early settlers.

The Publick Burying Ground

The story of the Publick Burying Ground begins in Doan's Corner which was part of the Township of East Cleveland. Doan's Corners was named after Nathaniel Doan (1762-1815) who came to the Western Reserve with the Connecticut Land Company in 1796. Nathaniel was a blacksmith by trade and was responsible for the care and maintenance of the horses used in the expeditions of the Connecticut Land Company. He purchased property and established a tavern/hotel and store that was located on the Northwest corner of what is now East 107th (formerly Shaker Road, later Fairmount Street) and Euclid Avenue. For the next eighty years this area of the city was known as Doan's Corner and served as a stopping place for those traveling between Cleveland and Buffalo. The travelers would stop and spend a day or two to rest before continuing on their journey.

It is not surprising that many began to settle in this area of Cuyahoga County located approximately four miles east of what we now know as downtown Cleveland. Keep in mind that at this point in time Cleveland only extended to what is now East 55th Street. The early settlers were frightened and rightfully so of the potential diseases they and their families would be exposed, such as malaria and cholera that tended to strike the low lying areas by the Cuyahoga River and lake. It was also the Doan's Corners area where the neighbors decided they would create a cemetery that was close to the townships of Euclid and Newburgh. This would not be the first cemetery in Cuyahoga County, that distinction belongs to what was known as Ontario Street Cemetery that was established in approximately 1820. Ontario Street Cemetery was closed by 1825 with many of the bodies removed to Erie Street Cemetery that is located on East 9th Street.

On November 11, 1822 the Doan's Corner neighbors met and committed to purchasing a share(s) in a cemetery that would cover the cost of the land to be purchased. The neighbors ultimately bought one acre of land from Judge John Harris Strong to be used as the Publick Burying Ground, which was located on Doan Street (now East 105th) and Euclid Avenue. Judge Strong was a prominent citizen of Cleveland arriving in approximately 1811 and was originally a land agent for those individuals still residing in Connecticut who owned large tracts of land in the Western Reserve/Cuyahoga County. Judge Strong settled in Euclid but was considered a resident of Cleveland due to his extensive business interests in Cleveland. Judge Strong was born in Middleton, Connecticut in 1762 the son of Deacon Josiah and Mary (nee Harris) Strong. He married Elizabeth Cary, Elizabeth being the sister of Timothy Doane's wife Mary Cary. Timothy and Mary Cary Doane arrived in Cleveland in 1802. Judge Strong and his wife brought with them to Cleveland their eight children, he became a Judge of the Common Pleas Court in Cuyahoga County in 1817 and served in that position until his death in 1823 at the age of 61 years. At one point in time Judge Strong owned all the land in Euclid and East Cleveland that was then located on the south side of Euclid Avenue between East 107th and East 79th Streets.[3]

As part of the process of purchasing the cemetery land the Burying Ground Society was formed, the articles of this Society were found to be as follows:

Articles for Burying Ground Society[4]

The subscribers, inhabitants of the east part of Cleaveland and the vicinity being desirous of establishing a publick burying ground, at or near Job Doan's, Esq.(Nathaniel Doan's son) *in said Cleaveland; and in order to accomplish so desirable a purpose, we the subjects hereby agree to pay the several sums annexed our names, for the purpose of purchasing one acre of land for the above purpose, and for a brick building, and we hereby agree to give several notes, for the sums by us subscribed in twenty days from date, payable to John Strong or order provided the land is purchased of said Strong. Each in the burying ground to own proportion to his subscription.*

Cleaveland, November 11th, 1822

Each of the thirty-three subscribers purchased a share(s) of the acre of land. The cost of the one acre lot was $40. The cost per share including surveying costs has been estimated to be approximately $1.20 per share, one share equaled one lot. The original subscribers were a diverse group of individuals some being more financially sound than others. This distinction is important as we will see this same diversity in the new East Cleveland Township Cemetery. The original thirty-three subscribers and the number of share(s) purchased by each subscriber are documented in Table 1.

In January of 1823, a meeting of the Burying Ground Society is documented confirming the purchase of the one-acre of land from Judge John H. Strong and the allocation of the lots based on the previously documented shares and their location in the cemetery. The recorded minutes of that meeting were as follows:

In a meeting held on Jan. 15th, 1823, chose Timothy Watkins, Chairman and Seth C. Baldwin Clerk – The Committee appointed for that purpose made report that they had received a deed of John H. Strong for the benefit of the society, and that they had surveyed the ground and divided the same agreeably to the plan here fore accepted by the society.

Voted the proprietors proceeded to a draft of the lots are now determined as follows: (See Table 2)

. . . . voted that a fence be built round the burying ground . . . the publick land, on the plan proposed by . . . .

=====================================

Hiram Baldwin purchased ½ of Lot 36 from Richard Kilbury on October 25, 1823 for 50 cents.

Lyman Rhodes purchased Joseph Butler on January 9, 1825.[5]

A map of the cemetery with the names of the lot owners still exists and has been redrawn in Figure 1. The map documents the cemetery as it was when it was closed in 1905 and contained two acres of land. Some of the names are faded and were unreadable. As you review the

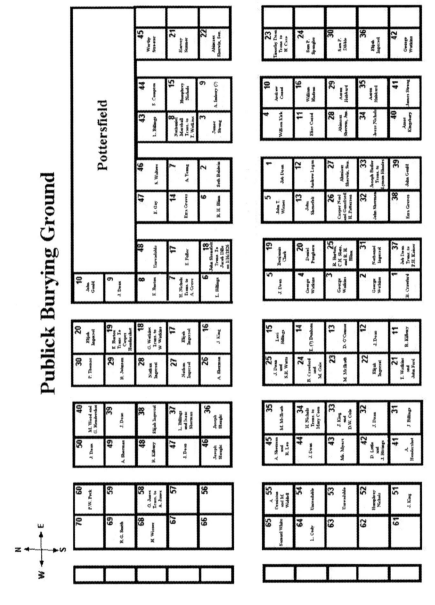

Figure 1

map, note that the original subscribers purchased lots in the East portion of the cemetery. The lots assigned to the thirty-three subscribers are documented in Table 2. The original one acre parcel was only on the East portion of the cemetery, with the West end of the original one acre running parallel with the West end of "Pottersfield." The western half of the cemetery was a second one acre parcel of land purchased in 1829.

The deed for the original parcel of land as noted above was signed on January 9, 1823; the deed was recorded on September 23, 1823 in Volume D, Page 530 reads as follows:

> *Do give, grant, bargain, sell, convey and confirm unto the said Aaron Hubbard, Job Doan and John Shenefelt who are appointed a committee by a number of persons living in the east part of said Cleaveland, and the north part of said Newburgh and the vicinity, who have associated together and signed articles for the purchase of a piece of land near Job Doan's in said Cleaveland **for the purpose of a burying ground and public buildings for the use and benefit of the subscribers**, and said committee shall from time to time quit claim so much of said land to each subscriber as shall be set off to his share or shares to be done at the expense of the receiver of said deed and what shall not be set off of said land as a burying ground shall remain in trust in the committee and their successors in office for the use and benefit of the subscribers for the purchase of said land, to be by them appropriated as above mentioned, a certain piece or parcel of land, being and lying in Cleaveland, Cuyahoga County, Ohio, bounded, beginning on the west line of the lot on which Job Doan now lives, running west on the north line of the road leading from Job Doan's to Cleaveland, 9 rods; thence Northwardly parallel with the west line of said Job Doan's lot as above mentioned, 20 rods to a stake; thence Eastwardly parallel with the road leading to Cleaveland as above mentioned, west line of the lot Southwardly 20 rods to the place of beginning, being a part of Lot No. 401 and containing 1 acre and 20 rods, but be it remembered and understood that 1 rod wide on*

the east of said track, the said Strong reserves for a public highway, if needed.

To have and to hold the above granted and bargained premises with the privileges and appurtenances therefore to them, the said Aaron Hubbard, Job Doan and John Shenefelt in their capacity as aforesaid and their successors in office for the purpose, use and benefit of the associates as aforesaid forever.

This deed is for the original one acre of land, the portion in bold print will become pivotal to the history of the Publick Burying Ground and will be clear later in the story.

On January 27, 1829 the Burying Ground Society purchased a second tract of land from Ezra Burns, a record of the deed could not be located. The property that is labeled "Second Purchase" was West of the original purchase on the survey performed by F.L. Krause on April 3, 1893. On December 21, 1829 the Burying Ground Society combined the two tracts of land.

Many of the first members of the Burying Ground Society's religious orientation were with the Presbyterian Church. As anti-slavery spread through the country, Cleveland was no exception, and many of the families had very strong anti-slavery views. The subscribers believed the Presbyterian Church, which was the prominent church at the time, was unable to take a broad enough stand against slavery and many of the families broke away from the Church and created what was then called the East Cleveland Congregational Church and later became known as the Euclid Avenue Congregational Church. The Burying Ground Society had originally documented that it would utilize a portion of the one-acre of land to build a brick building. Construction of the brick building for the church began in 1844 and was completed in 1846. The last documented meeting of the Burying Ground Society was made on March 12, 1834. The record of this meeting was recorded as follows:

Cleveland, March 12th, 1834. The society met at the home of Job Doan – agreeable notices. The meeting began by calling Elijah Ingersoll, to the chair; a motion for elections where Humphrey

Nichols, Andrew Cozad and Elias Cozad were elected committee; Timothy W. Watkins, Treasurer and Michael Kilbury, Saxton and Job Doan clerk for the ensuing year.

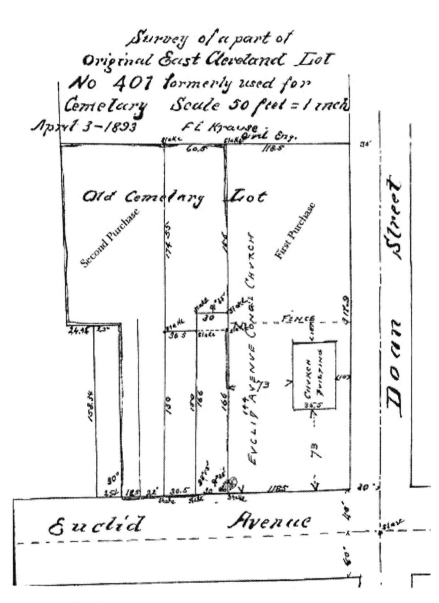

The Western Reserve Historical Society, Cleveland, Ohio

The original subscribers to the Publick Burying Ground were some of the first settlers in the Western Reserve. To put this into perspective, consider the 1820 estimated population of Cuyahoga County was 150 people. The thirty-three men who worked together to create the Publick Burying Ground represented approximately 22% of the population at that time. It seems fitting that we remember a few of them at this juncture, with biographical information of the others in Remembering Our Early Settlers.

Seth Cogswell Baldwin came to Cleveland in 1817 from Ballston Springs, New York with his eight children. Prior to his arrival in Cleveland, Mr. Baldwin served during the American Revolution with Ethan Allan at Ticonderoga, and subsequently served under Colonel Grosvenor. The Battle of Ticonderoga occurred on May 10, 1775, Ethan Allen, an American Revolutionary soldier, led his Green Mountain Boys in an attack to overtake the fort. These soldiers seized Fort Ticonderoga and all of its valuable artillery stores without a struggle. The name Ticonderoga comes from the Iroquois Indian word *Cheonderoga*, meaning "place between two waters."

He was also a pioneer settler of Ballston Springs, New York. Mr. Baldwin held important public positions in Ballston Springs, namely, Supervisor in 1793 and 1800-1801; Member of the Assembly for the period of 1797 thru 1799; was Sheriff for the period of 1801 thru 1803; and was County Clerk for the years 1804 to 1813.[6]

Mr. Baldwin's wife passed away in 1805 after the birth of their daughter, Ruth White Baldwin, who was named after her mother. Mr. Baldwin married a second time to Abigail Kellogg Baldwin. They had two children. The second Mrs. Baldwin passed away a year after the family's arrival in Cleveland.

During Mr. Baldwin's brief time in Cleveland, he took on the role of surveyor. He was responsible for surveying many of the farms in the township and a large portion of Cuyahoga County.

Mr. Baldwin passed away on September 28, 1828 and is now buried in East Cleveland Township Cemetery in Section 12, Lot 21. The Early Settlers' Association of Cuyahoga County wrote the following:

Mr. Seth Baldwin, was a man of wealth and influence, conspicuous in the political and social life of his day. He lived in a large colonial mansion in the center of an extensive farm worked by many slaves. He had been a soldier in the War of the Revolution, serving under Ethan Allen at the taking of Fort Ticonderoga. Subsequently he enlisted under Colonel Grosvenor, grandfather of Gen. Charles Grosvenor of Ohio. His home was the center of great hospitality, and carriages preceded by outriders frequently arrived at his doors, laden with guests from Schenectady, Albany and other Eastern cities. Large parties often spent weeks at a time visiting at his home.

By indorsing for friends and through the repudiation of the Continental currency, he lost his fortune, and resolved to move to the great West, coming to Cleveland in 1817. He located at Doan's Corners, then a struggling frontier settlement. In his new home, Mr. Baldwin adopted the occupation of surveyor, and many of the farms throughout this county were staked out and surveyed by him. He was regarded as a very valuable citizen, and did everything in his power to promote the interests of the new settlement.[7]

Elias Cozad was born May 6, 1790 in Mendham, Morris County, New Jersey and came to Cleveland with his parents, Samuel, Jr. and Jane (nee McIlrath) Cozad in approximately 1806. Elias, and his brother Andrew were, according to the family, descendants of Jacques Cossart, a Huguenot who fled from La Rochelle, France to Leyden, Holland and from there sailed on the ship Der Pumerlander Kerck and arrived in New Amsterdam (Manhattan Island) on October 14, 1662.

Elias' home was located on Euclid Avenue near the current entrance to Lake View Cemetery. Elias married Hannah Palmer before 1814; she was the daughter of Thomas and Sarah (nee Fordyce) Palmer. Elias and Hannah had five children, Cynthia L, Julia Ann, Ethan A.B., Amelia H and Aurilla. Elias laid the cornerstone for the first tannery in Cleveland on March 29, 1810 which was located where Adelbert College of Western Reserve University was later erected; now where Adelbert Hall of Case Western Reserve University still stands today.

> *Elias Cozad laid the cornerstone of his tannery at Doan's Cor-*
> *ners, the first to be built in the district later known as Cleveland.*
> *Trappers brought him raw furs of wolves, foxes, bears, and squir-*
> *rels, which, when tanned and dressed, provided leather for makers*
> *of boots and shoes in the community.*[8]

Elias was a veteran of the War of 1812 serving as an Ensign; 1st Regiment, 4th Brigade; 4th Division, Ohio Militia.

Elias passed away in 1880 at the age of 90 years, and is buried in Section 6, Lot 1 in East Cleveland Township Cemetery along with his wife, Hannah, and their children, Ethan Allen, Amelia, Cynthia and Julia.

Job Doan (Doane) was born in 1785 in Chatham, Connecticut and was the only son of Nathaniel and Sarah (nee Adams) Doan. After Nathaniel's death in 1815, Job rebuilt the Doan Tavern replacing the log tavern with a large frame tavern. Job was described as an energetic, ambitious, hard-working man. Note should be made that Nathaniel and Timothy Doane were brothers. Timothy's family continued to spell their surname as Doane, whereas Nathanial's family dropped the "e" on the end.

Job married Harriett Woodruff, the daughter of Nathaniel and Isabelle Woodruff of Morristown, New Jersey. They had eight children prior to Job's untimely death of cholera in 1834. Many members of the Timothy Doane family can be found in East Cleveland Township Cemetery.

Job Doan passed away on September 20, 1834. His obituary in the *Cleveland Whig* on September 24, 1834 read as follows:

> *Job Doan, a well-known politician died of cholera on the*
> *morning of Sept. 20. He was a respectable man and a kind father.*
> *His death will be mourned by many.*

After his death, his wife Harriett married Cornelius Conkley. Harriett died in 1884. Records indicate she is buried in Lake View Cemetery.

Job was transferred from the Publick Burying Ground on May 9, 1876 to Lake View Cemetery, Section 8, Lot 90.

Timothy Watkins and his wife Sophia (nee Heard) came to Cleveland in 1814 with several of their children; other children followed their arrival in Cleveland. There were six children born to the marriage. Upon their arrival the family bought their farm on Euclid Avenue and suffered extreme poverty for several years. Their first winter in Cleveland was very difficult as their log home had only three sides with the fourth side open to the wind and weather. Mr. Watkins was the first Chairman of the Publick Burying Ground. When Mr. and Mrs. Watkins passed away, they were originally buried in the Publick Burying Ground. The family members buried in the Publick Burying Ground were removed to the East Cleveland Township Cemetery and can be found in Section 2, Lot 37.

Timothy Watkins' son, George Watkins will play a major role in the history of the cemetery in later years. The church continued to grow and by the end of the Civil War plans were in progress to build a larger church, at another site which still exists today at the corner of Logan (now East 96th Street) and Euclid Avenues.

One of the urban legends surrounding the history of the East Cleveland Township Cemetery revolved around the people buried in the cemetery who had passed away very early in Cleveland's history. The records located clearly document that the deaths that occurred prior to the East Cleveland Township Cemetery coming into existence were in fact transferred from the Publick Burying Ground or elsewhere. The Publick Burying Ground has also been referred to over the years as, the cemetery across from Job Doan's tavern, the East Cleveland burying ground (late 1800's), Doan's Corner Cemetery (currently) and the little cemetery on Euclid Avenue. In early Cleveland, it was not uncommon to move the bodies of family members from one cemetery to another, to move them from a family burial plot on a farm to a cemetery or from the west side of Cleveland to the east side as families immigrated across the City.

The burial records of the Publick Burying Ground are scarce and incomplete; and it is this status of the records that supports the reported fact that the Publick Burying Ground Society had been gradually disappearing and by 1834 the records were no longer being maintained, despite ongoing burials. The paper on which the burial records were documented has deteriorated to the point that the pages are crumbling and the writing has faded, what is still readable is listed below.[9] Death notices were located in the *Cleveland Herald* for several of the people listed in the burial records and that information along with the date the notice appeared in the newspaper is contained below the name.

1. *?? Rhodes son of Lyman Rhodes died February ?, 1827, age 1 year.*
2. *Ann Eliza Strong died March 19th, 1827, aged 26 years.*
    March 23, 1827: Died in Cleveland township on Mar. 19, 1827, Mrs. Ann Eliza Strong, 26, wife of James Strong. Mrs. Strong was the daughter of Seth C. Baldwin, Esq., formerly of Ballstown, N.Y.
3. *?? Billings, Electa Ann Billings and an infant child son and ? of Levi Billings removed to the burying ground ??? 27th, 1827.*
4. *Nehemiah Wallace died July 6th, 1828, aged 25 years.*
    July 11, 1828: Died, in Newburgh, on the 6th inst., Mr. Nehemiah Wallace, aged 65 years, formerly from Shoreham, Vermont.
5. *Lyman Rhodes died January 10th, 1828 aged ___ years.*
    January 18, 1828: Died, in Newburgh, Jan. 10, Lyman Rhodes; leaving a disconsolate wife and four small children to deplore their loss.
6. *Timothy Doan died April 3, 1828 aged _____ years.*
7. *?? Niles died April 15, 1828, age 55 years.*
8. *Hannah Sherwin died June 26, 1828 aged 32 years.* July 4, 1828: *Died, on the 26th ult., Mrs. Hannah Sherwin, wife of Ahimaz Sherwin, Jr., of this village, aged 32.*
9. *?? Scott died August 29, 1828 aged 20 years.*
10. *?? Harris died September 3, 1828 age 34 years.*
11. *Anna Cozad died September 14, 1828 age 23 years.*
12. *Seth C. Baldwin died September 12, 1828 age 66 years.*
    September 26, 1828: Died, in this village, on Sept. 18, Seth C. Baldwin, Esq., a soldier of the revolution, aged 66 years. Printers in Saratoga county, New York, please insert the above.

13. *N. Clark Cozad died September 23, 1828 age 24 years.*
14. *John Riddell died January 17, 1829 age 40 years.*
15. *Hudson died March 3, 1829 son of William Hudson, age 20 years.*
16. *??cia Baker died March 14, 1829 wife of Alpeus Baker age ____.*
17. *John Welch Jr. son of John Welch died July 19th, 1829 age 6 months.*
18. *Jane Celestia Cozad daughter of Andrew Cozad died August 7, 1829 aged 3 years.*
19. *Benjamin Hathaway died October 24, 1829 age 66 years.*

October 29, 1829: *Died. At the house of Mr. Ahimaz Sherwin in Cleaveland, Ohio, on the 24th of Oct. inst., Mr. Benjamin Hathaway, late of Hartland, Vermont.*

20. *Son of Laban Ingersoll died November 22, 1829 age 16 months.*
21. *Lorenzo Eddy son of Dennis Eddy died December 17, 1829 age 5 years.*
22. *Harriett Kidwell died January 28, 1830.*
23. *Russell Wheeler died April 3, 1830 age 26 years.*

July 8, 1830: *At the anniversary of the declaration of independence, celebrated at the house of Job Doan, in this town, on July 5, a revolutionary soldier by the name of Wheeler is supposed to have eaten so much as to cause his death, as he was found dead the next day.*

The arrow of fate seems directed particularly at this family of Wheelers, as a son of the deceased was killed a few days since, by the bursting of a swivel, while 'a few of the strongest party' were rejoicing over the election of a Jacksonian of this town, for justice of the peace.

24. *Walter Miller died July 6, 1830.*
25. *Timothy Watkins died September 2, 1830, aged 57 years.*
26. *Hasen Dibble son of S. Dibble died October 20, 1830.*
27. *Eber Sawtell son of J. Sawtell died October 3, 1830.*
28. *Ann Olmsted died November 17, 1830.*

In 1844 there is a report that the "*proprietors of the public ground adjoining and south of the burying ground*" deeded the property to the trustees of the First Presbyterian Society for a church and "*the necessary appendages thereto.*" On this property the Euclid Avenue Congregational Church was founded.[10] Before the church was built, the deceased would be taken into the school house and from there to their place of rest.

Euclid Avenue Congregational Church
Photograph by Henry M. Ladd

The Burying Ground Society faded away and was not heard from again until George Watkins (1812-1902), John R. Walters (1811-1886) and Judge John W. Heisley (1823-1893) joined together on behalf of the Burying Ground Society, on or about 1842. These three men began making plans to buy the interests of the previously purchased lots from the original owners or their heirs in the Publick Burying Ground. John R. Walters passed away in 1886 and is buried in the East Cleveland Township Cemetery, Section 3, Lot 19; and John W. Heisley passed away in 1893, it is believed that he is buried in Lake View Cemetery with his wife, Elizabeth Keller Heisley.

On November 21, 1859, immediately after the creation of the East Cleveland Township Cemetery, the first recorded transfers from the Publick Burying Ground were moved to East Cleveland Township Cemetery. They were Dr. Elijah Burton and Mary Burton, followed by Frances and Helen Post on January 27, 1860. There are at least 75 people that are securely documented in the burial records of East Cleveland Township Cemetery as having been transferred from the Publick Burying Ground. It is believed that many more than those clearly documented were transferred from the Publick Burying Ground. It was George Watkins, John R. Walters and John W. Heisley who coordinated the effort to move the people buried in the Publick Burying Ground to East Cleveland Township Cemetery.

In 1930 Charles Asa Post writes of the removal of the bodies from the Publick Burying Ground:

> *Some of the Corners victims of the cholera scourges of 1832 and 1834 were interred in the old cemetery back of the churches, and when building encroachments necessitated the removal of all the remains to another cemetery, there was some discussion as to the danger of infection from opening the graves, but nothing of the sort resulted.*
>
> *Mrs. Clara Ford Gould has reminded me that when this wholesale removal from the cemetery occurred some of the coffins were found to have been covered with leather or rawhide, studded with brass or copper nails, and showing the name and date.*[11]

The motivation behind these efforts became apparent on February 3, 1894, at least 50 years later, when George Watkins on behalf of the Trustees of the Burying Ground Association filed suit against the Euclid Avenue Congregational Church, bearing Cuyahoga County Common Pleas case numbers 48218 and 48219.[12] In these cases Watkins, et al alleged that as a "Trustee of the Burying Ground Association" he had legal right of ownership of the cemetery and adjoining property rather than the Euclid Avenue Congregational Church.

The author believes that the property description outlined in Cuyahoga County Common Pleas case number 48218 contained errors and may have been the basis for Watkins' decision to dismiss the action. The property description in the two Common Pleas cases (48218 and 48219) were very different. Cuyahoga County Common Pleas case number 48219 survived and was ultimately transferred to Circuit Court where the matter was tried.[13]

These two acres of land had become quite valuable. Watkins and his partners had worked many years to disinter and transfer the bodies of the deceased elsewhere. The entrepreneurial spirit of these three men was unique. The records do not indicate that the Publick Burying Ground issued individual deeds to the cemetery lots sold as became the practice with subsequent cemeteries. Cemeteries created later in time utilized cemetery lot deeds, this practice was in place by at least 1859 when East Cleveland Township Cemetery came into existence. The cemetery lot deeds specifically indicated the lot was being sold for burial purposes only. It was this lack of clear documentation regarding ownership rights in the cemetery lot that Watkins and his partners were attempting to utilize to their benefit.

With the lack of documentation that the cemetery lots were sold for the purpose of burials only, Watson and his partners began to purchase the cemetery lots from the original subscriber's heirs. They were attempting to get ownership of the lots and thereafter remove the bodies with the idea that once they had full ownership of all the cemetery lots, they would be the rightful owners of the property were the cemetery was located at what is now East 105th and Euclid Avenue.

One of the witnesses at the Circuit Court trial concerning the ownership of the cemetery was Horace Ford (1823-1905). Horace Ford was the uncle of Horatio Clark Ford (1853-1915) who had been working on obtaining clear title to the property for the Euclid Avenue Congregational Church. Horace Ford was a well respected citizen of Cuyahoga County. Mr. Ford's parents Cyrus and Clarissa Whitmarsh Ford arrived in Cleveland in 1837. Cyrus gave the family farm, which consisted of 200 acres of land, to Horace. Horace had worked the family farm during the summer months and taught school in the winters. Horace was also a charter member of the Euclid Avenue Congregational Church, taught Sunday school for the church and was also appointed a Deacon.

In an effort to visualize the testimony of Horace Ford provided during the course of the Circuit Court trial, note should be made of Figure 2. There was a fence built around the cemetery that J. A. Post assisted in constructing. Prior to 1860 if a funeral procession came from Euclid Avenue it could enter off Euclid Avenue, after the construction of the fence the funeral procession would turn down Doan Street and enter through the "Main Alley" of the cemetery. The "Main Alley" was 10 feet wide and each of the walkways shown in the diagram were 7 feet wide. Each lot in the cemetery was 16-1/2 feet square, with each lot holding approximately 6 single graves. However, because there were no rules or regulations regarding the stacking of graves, which was a common practice up until recently, each lot could have accommodated more than 6 burials. "*There was no regular drive-way ever made across the commons to Euclid avenue. As long as it was not fenced they drove in any direction. But after 1870 all processions, funerals and vehicles passed in from the Doan street entrance.*" The hitching posts were described as having a spiked rail on top of the posts and the horses were hitched to the rail. The hitching posts were located approximately six feet from the fence and ran parallel with the fence and were utilized by the Disciple Church and the East Cleveland Congregational Church (now the Euclid Avenue Congregational Church). The fence around the cemetery had a main gate off Doan Street, and two smaller gates one in front of the Disciple Church and the other in front of the Euclid Avenue Congregational Church.[14]

The lawsuit filed by Watkins did not result in the finding he and his partners had worked towards for many years. Portions of Judge J.B. Burrows' decision of February 21, 1896, in the Circuit Court case were as follows:

Now it would be useless to go over the history of this land and its use and occupation for the number of years--70 years and more--and I will only advert to two or three questions. One is, the position that this plaintiff occupies. Is he a trustee, and as such can he maintain this suit? The conveyance was made to Hubbard, Doan and Shenefelt in 1823 and to their successors in office,--those that

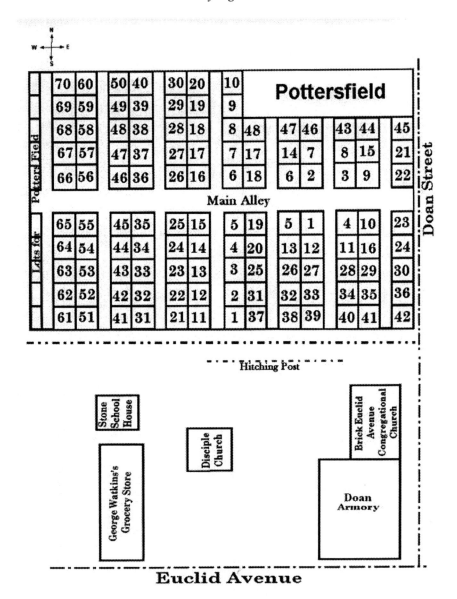

Figure 2

should be committeemen appointed thereafter for the owners of
this land or contributors to the fund. While these parties originally
committeemen were appointed in 1823, the evidence shows either

by death or resignation that a meeting was held in 1842, and there was a new committee appointed by the Association–Samuel Baldwin, J. R. Walters and George Watkins. There never has been a meeting of that Association since, so far as the evidence shows. There has never been any appointment of any committees since. The only survivor of that committee is George Watkins the plaintiff. We are not quite certain what rights he has a committeeman. Perhaps if we were compelled to place our decision upon that ground, we might be able to find that the evidence was clear and satisfactory that he was appointed as committeeman by that association. He himself testifies that there was a meeting and that there was some record in a book but he doesn't say how many of the members of that association were present; and since that time I think he has done no act in furtherance of the trust, if he was made a committeeman at that time and accepted the trust. But I say we are not disposed to put the decision upon that ground.

In 1844 a contract was made or a lease (or as it is called, a deed) to the church of this very land for the purpose of erecting a house of worship. This committeeman signed this lease not as a committeeman or a trustee, but as an individual–his father was one of the members of the Association, and I think it appears perhaps that he had at that time some interest in these lands. Now, I have said it does not appear that he had done anything in execution of this trust. He did make a lease to Mr. Doan in 1877 with his associates for a year. But that was after he commenced purchasing shares or the rights of the members in this association, and apparently in his interest as an individual, and not as a trustee to hold possession of this land. At any rate, under this deed he had no authority to make the lease. The land that is south of the burying ground shall remain in trust and what shall not be set off of said land as a burying ground—the land that is south of the burying ground shall remain in trust in the committee and successors in office for the use and benefit of the subscribers to be by them appropriated for public buildings. Not by the trustees. The trustees have no right to appropriate it. I cannot see how the trustees had any right to make a lease except that they were directed by the members of the association. If under this deed he was a trustee, he was a trustee simply and only for the purpose of holding the naked legal title and nothing else. Everything in respect to it that was to be done to this south part was under the control by the deed itself of the members of the association. The trustees had nothing to do with it, and so they acted when they gave the privilege or the deed or whatever it may be denominated to the church to put up the house for public worship.

Now the first question that we reach in this case is the question of the plaintiff's possession at the time of the commencement of this suit, and here we are not satisfied that the plaintiff's contention is correct. He says he was in possession at the time of the commencement of this suit as trustee. Manifestly he ceased long ago to act as trustee for anybody but himself and his associates. And whatever was done in payment of building sidewalks, or anything else that was done, Mr. Heisley and himself and the other trustee while he was living I believe, J.R. Walters, each contributed one-third of their own money for their own benefit. He was not attempting to hold it for the members of the society, but was attempting simply to hold and control it for the purpose of getting the title to himself and his co-partners in the transaction.

Now if we admit that that is so--we are assuming that he is a trustee bringing this suit as trustee--his testimony shows that it is simply a fiction, that the suit is not brought in good faith as a trustee for the benefit of the trust, but he is using his office (if it be an office) his capacity as trustee simply to accomplish another purpose. For he says if he succeeds in this suit that he expects to divide the property between the estate of Mr. Heisley and himself. He says that upon the stand. That he does not expect to get this property by this suit for the purposes of the cestui que trust. Now it is replied to this that that does not matter, that does not concern this defendant, what his ultimate object or purpose may be, and probably that is correct that if he is really a trustee and gets possession of it those in interest can compel him to execute his trust or remove him and have some other party appointed. But it does concern the Court if it does not concern the defendants; and we think the rule is well settled that a court will not aid a party who comes into court pretending to act as trustee when he confesses that he is using it for another and different purpose only, and we would be disposed to take the position upon this ground and dismiss the petition because he is not bringing this suit in good faith as a trustee for the benefit of his trust.[15]

Judge Burrows was quoted by the *Cleveland Leader* as stating:

But one thing seems certain in this case, and that is that all of you gentlemen are right, and that is the decision I am forced to reach. All of the claimants are right in saying that none of the others owns the property. Therefore, no one owns it.[16]

It is believed that Judge Burrows may have had access to an agreement between George Watkins, John W. Heisley and John R. Walters that was signed and dated May 6, 1876, in addition to the testimony Judge Burrow's referenced that was given by George Watkins at trial. The agreement read as follows:

This is to show that we are jointly engaged in buying up interests in the Burying Ground in Lot 401 in the 17th Ward of Cleveland, Ohio and agree each to pay one third interest of any money paid or that shall be paid out by either for that purpose each of us having a one third interest in what is or shall be purchased.

Judge Burrows concluded that Watkins was acting on his behalf and not as a Trustee of the Publick Burying Ground Society. The self-interest attested to in the private agreement negated the idea that Watkins, Heisley and Walters acted on behalf of the Society. As no one represented the interests of the Society, the Society no longer existed in the eyes of the Court and as a result no one owned the land or the lots in the Publick Burying Ground.

In October 1898 a resolution was introduced to the City of Cleveland common council requesting that the cemetery property located on the corner of Euclid Avenue and Doan Street be held in trust for the public. The resolution further requested that property be utilized for an art gallery or high school building. The Council committee voted against this resolution. An article in the *Cleveland Leader* on October 4, 1898 reported the following:

> *The committee decided that inasmuch as the property had been deeded for a specific purpose to the trustees of an association, the city had no right to it, and had never exercised any authority over it. Therefore the committee decided to make an adverse report on the resolution.*

This article concluded that this act of the committee narrowed the potential owners of the property to the Euclid Avenue Congregational Church and Echo M. Heisley, Esq. (the son of John W. Heisley). It further reports that the market value of the property in question was $50,000.

Cleveland Press Collection – Cleveland Public Library

The issue concerning ownership continued into the future with the Grand Army of the Republic creating a "Secret Committee" to attempt to gain possession of the property, which in 1901, was valued between $100,000 and $200,000. The Forest City Post of the G.A.R. had been using the small brick addition to the old church for a number of years. The lawsuits concerning the Publick Burying Ground land was a standing joke of the Cleveland Bar, it was said to be a local parallel of Dickens' famous case of *Jarndyce and Jarndyce*. In 1898 there was also a movement to utilize the property for a public library.[17]

According to George Watkins, by March, 1899 all the bodies in the Publick Burying Ground had been removed except for seven, which were in fact many of the Roldolphus Edwards, Sr. family. Mr. Watkins reported to the Euclid Avenue Congregational Church during a meeting held on March 28, 1899 that a member of the Edwards' family, a carpenter by trade, had frequently threatened that he would shoot him if he undertook removal of the bodies of the Edwards family that were buried around the family monument.

During the course of the meeting, Mr. Watkins indicated that there were four or five members of the Edwards family, the body of Lyman Rhodes and the body of Philinda Gould (Section 6, Lot 36), the wife of John Gould which had not yet been removed. All of these individuals can be located in the East Cleveland Township Cemetery along with the Edwards monument. What is interesting about the Gould family is that the East Cleveland Township Cemetery burial records indicate they were transferred into East Cleveland Township Cemetery on March 25, 1864, which would seem to indicate that Mr. Watkins' records were not necessarily accurate.

The article below, *"Tavern Keeper Lost Loved Ones Within Three Years. Mother, Father, Wife and Daughter All Died–He was Buried Beside Them Seven Years Later–Mute Testimony of Time-Worn Stones"* tells the story of the Edwards' family and the Publick Burying Ground:[18]

> *Hewn with infinite pains from the native rock, it was the finest monument in all the cemetery. It was always the largest; now it is almost the last. With two smaller slabs of stone it stands in the*

*Edwards Family Monument
– Author Photograph Collection*

little common behind the old church building on the northwest corner of Euclid-av and Doan-st. Boys play marbles on the very graves; they frolic beneath the spreading elm; they play ball and chalk their scores on the monument itself. The pride of the churchyard has become a plaything of children.

Boys played there half a century ago. Released from the Doan's Corner district school, in what was then the village of East Cleveland, they crossed the street to play hide and seek among the graves. Though they might, unintentionally in their romping, step upon a grave, they never thought of defacing a gravestone, least of all the then imposing monument put there by Rodolphus Edwards, who kept the old Buckeye tavern at what is now the corner of Woodland and Woodland Hills-avs, and was a man of mark.

The school house is still there, but it is now a part of engine house 10 and firemen sleep in it. The old church, built in pride by members of the Euclid-av Congregational church in 1844, is now a carpenter shop in part and in part a hall in which meets Forest City Post, Grand Army of the Republic, and once a week a little party gathers in prayer meeting. The front entrance, once an architectural triumph, has long been closed. The yard is littered and boarded from view.

Thirty years ago the church society built its present home at Euclid and Logan and left the corner where its members had par-

ticipated in the stirring scenes of wartime. The building is still owned by the church and the prayer meetings are held there, it is said, to keep the title unimpaired. But the rentals are nominal and the property is too valuable to be left practically unoccupied. So it is like to be sold soon, and the old church will follow the cemetery into oblivion.

The East Cleveland burying ground, as it was called in those days, fronted on Doan-st and extended back some distance parallel with Euclid-av. The entrance was from Doan-st and, as usual, comparatively few graves were dug near it.

The Edwards monument was given its prominent place for its magnificence and the standing of the Edwards family. There have been no burials in the old cemetery since the civil war and most of the graves were opened long since and their contents and tombstones moved to the newer East Cleveland cemetery opposite Lake View.

For a dozen years the Edwards monument and its two smaller companions have stood alone and neglected. Rodolphus Edwards, its builder and the keeper of the famous tavern, is not buried there, it is said, but the old stone bears witness to his long life and his death, thus: "Rodolphus Edwards eldest son of Adonijah & Polly Edwards, was born Jan. 26, 1759 and died July 17, 1840." On the same face of the stone is this record of the tavern keeper's wife: "Anna, wife of Rodolphus Edwards, died June 19, 1833, in the 54th year of her age." The south side of the stone has this to say of Rodolphus Edwards' parents: "Adonijah Edwards was born Sept. 27, 1741 and died Jan. 9, 1831," and this: "Polly, wife of Adonijah Edwards, died Feb. 18, 1832 in the 88th year of her age."

The short life of Rodolphus Edwards' daughter is recorded on the north face: "Anna, wife of Noble Olmsted & daughter of Rodolphus and Anna Edwards, died Nov. 17, 1830, aged 25 years."

So Rodolphus Edwards lost his mother, his father, and his daughter within three years and survived them all by seven.

The grave of another Edwards is but a few feet from the monument. Its simple stone bears this legend: "Rhoda Edwards, widow of Lyman Rhoades, wife of Benajah Fay, born March 10, 1798, *died March 29, 1859." Between this stone and the Edwards monument stands a battered slab that was considered something elaborate in its day, with a bough of "weeping willow" drooping over an urn chiseled at the top. The willow testifies to the grief of Rhoda Edwards for her first husband for the inscription says: "In memory of Lyman Rhoades." There are other words, but they are illegible now. The Italic lettering has been gradually effaced from the weather-beaten stone.*

The branch of the Edwards family descended from the old tavern keeper is said to be scattered. The stone that was once his pride, though insignificant nowadays, seems to command no respect. The graves are sunken, the mounds have disappeared. Rodolphus Edwards and his family seem to have gone from the member of present generations as completely as his famous old Buckeye tavern.

The records compiled by George Watkins and the Euclid Avenue Congregational Church are documented in Table 3. These records were submitted by George Watkins to Horatio Clark Ford and T.S. Knight as representatives of the Euclid Avenue Congregational Church to document the money expended to purchase the various lots in the Publick Burying Ground; to document ownership of the cemetery lots; and, the costs associated with the removal of the bodies. After Watkins submitted his records to the Euclid Avenue Congregational Church, the Church attempted to verify Watkins' records. In several cases there are variances between Watkins' ledger and the handwritten notes transferring ownership of the cemetery lots to Watkins' and/or his partners, John R. Walters and John W. Heisley. The handwritten notes transferring lot ownership were often times groups of unrelated individual heirs as documented in Figure 3.

It is believed that the variance in the monies paid and recorded in Watkins' ledger included the costs associated with removal of the bodies in addition to the cost of purchasing the individual cemetery lots. The compilation of the records of George Watkins and those of the Euclid Avenue Congregational Church supports the fact that many of the burials in the Publick Burying Ground can be traced to East Cleveland Township Cemetery.

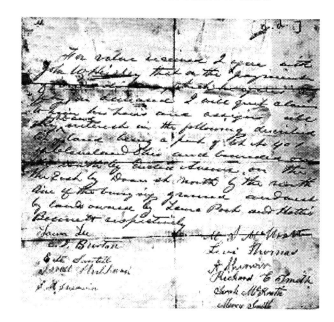

Figure 3 The Western Reserve Historical Society, Cleveland, Ohio

In the records of the Publick Burying Ground Society a map with the names of the lot owners written in each lot block was utilized to trace the owners and/or their families from the Publick Burying Ground. The information from the map was compared to the East Cleveland Township Cemetery burial records, and the records of several other cemeteries, the results are located in Table 4.

The burial records of the East Cleveland Township Cemetery also clearly document in many cases those people transferred from the Publick Burying Ground, which by 1859 was referred to as Doan's Corner Cemetery. Table 5 documents these transfers, the reference to a Section, Lot, etc. are the location in East Cleveland Township Cemetery where these people were interred.

There is also another group of individuals transferred to East Cleveland Township Cemetery where the records indicate they were transferred from other areas of Cleveland and "Private Ground" (Table 6). "Private Ground" could refer to family burial plots on family land, but it could also refer to the Publick Burying Ground. For example, we know Elias Cozad and Timothy Watkins both owned lots in the Publick

Burying Ground and their family members who died prior to 1859 are now interred in East Cleveland Township Cemetery.

There is an urban legend speculating East Cleveland Township Cemetery existed prior to 1859. The information compiled in the Tables indicates the urban legend is without merit. The first recorded burial in East Cleveland Township Cemetery was Mr. Duncan, who was 83 years of age at the time of his death on August 31, 1859. His residence on the burial record indicates he was from Pennsylvania. To further document that the East Cleveland Township Cemetery came into existence in 1859 will be further explored in the following chapter where we review the ownership of the property that became East Cleveland Township Cemetery.

There were stories regarding what became of a number of the headstones from the Publick Burying Ground. In 1930 Charles Asa Post recounted the following:

> *The proprietor of the first bakery at the Corners came soon after the old Cemetery was abolished and the remains removed, and while there were still some portions of ancient broken gravestones scattered about. It was said that he used some of these fragments of stone for the bottom of his bake oven, so that his loaves sometime had imprinted upon them reminders of the long departed.*[19]

The other recounted story is:

> *It has been reported that the thrifty Mr. Watkins operated a grocery store west of the corners and that the walk leading up to his door was paved with the various and sundry tombstones, laid face down.*[20]

A short time after the March 28, 1899 meeting, Mr. Watkins conveyed his entire interest in the Publick Burying Ground land, which included the previous interest of J.R. Walters to the Church for $2,500. Lillian, Samuel and Echo M. Heisley, heirs of John W. Heisley, were paid $2,500 in 1900 and another $2,500 was paid to Echo M. Heisley in 1901.

These payments along with all costs, taxes on the property, expenses of the lawsuits, costs related to the deed and other items were paid by Horatio Clark Ford. There had been a previous agreement between Mr. Ford and the Church, wherein Mr. Ford agreed to obtain a clear title to the land and would thereafter be reimbursed for the costs by the Church.

S. J. Kelly wrote of the litigation as follows:

> *Clouds of litigation, which had been gathering between the Euclid Avenue Congregational Church and the cemetery owners and trustees, burst into a storm in 1890. This was to continue for 13 years. In 1899 Doan deeded the armory to the church, and by 1905 the Congregationalists had clear deed to a long, valuable tract leading north on E. 105*[th] *Street and covering the bank site on the corner of Euclid and the Alhambra Theater lot, which was sold to the Cleveland Trust Co. The armory was torn down and in the fall of 1906 the old Congregational Church was leveled to the ground.*[21]

The front portion of the land that was one of the earliest cemeteries in the Cleveland area was sold to the Cleveland Trust Company in October of 1905 for $40,000 by the Euclid Avenue Congregational Church; the back portion was leased to the Cleveland Trust Company for 50 years and subsequently sold to this organization in 1941 for $60,000 by the Euclid Avenue Congregational Church. The monies obtained from the lease and sale of this land were utilized by the Church to create an endowment which continues to assist in the financial support of the Church to this day.

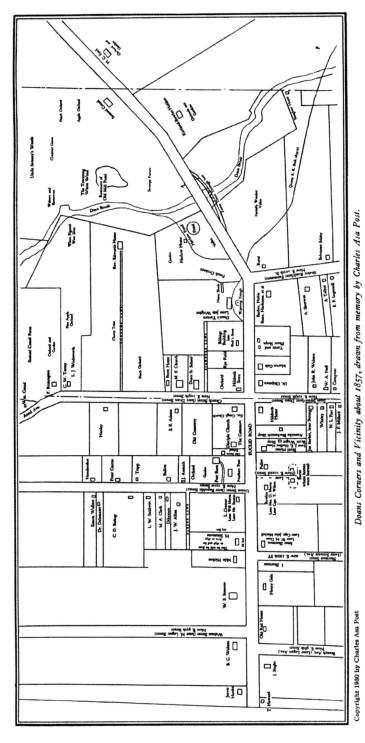

Doans Corners and Vicinity about 1857, drawn from memory by Charles Asa Post.
Revised from County Map by C. H. Hutchinson.

Charles Asa Post passed away on May 2, 1943 and is buried in East Cleveland Township Cemetery, Section 1.1 ot 23

East Cleveland Township Cemetery ≈ The Land

For this portion of our journey we need to understand that when the Connecticut Land Company surveyed the land in the Western Reserve which included what is now Cuyahoga County, they did so in 10 and 100 acre lots of land. The land division looked much like a large grid that contained squares of 10 and 100 acre lots; each of these lots was then assigned a unique number.

The urban legend as it relates to the property on which the East Cleveland Township Cemetery resides is based on an assumption that the land had previously been used as a family burial plot, and thus proved its existence prior to 1859. This assumption is flawed based on the documentation provided in the previous chapter wherein it was documented that Andrew Cozad owned a burial lot in the Publick Burying Ground. The urban legend is also not supported by the multiple sales of the land that eventually became the East Cleveland Township Cemetery. A reasonable person would need to assume that if Cozad family members were buried on any part of this property, they would not have sold the land. Also the land would not have been sold as frequently as it was prior to being purchased by the Trustees of East Cleveland Township.

Some have attempted to make a case that the 1852 map of Cuyahoga County that documents lot number 396 with a triangle located on the north side of Euclid Avenue indicated the potential existence of the cemetery. However, one must look deeper and review the actual deeds to the property to determine if the land was being utilized as a cemetery.

Portion of 1858 Map of Cuyahoga County, Lot Number 396

Because of the urban legends regarding the cemetery land, research began by tracing the property ownership back to the Connecticut Land Company. On June 28, 1802 Samuel Cozad, Jr. purchased lots numbered 40, 41, 42, 43, 50 to 61 inclusive, 64 to 69 inclusive, 83 to 94 inclusive, 99 to 111 inclusive, and parts of one-hundred acre lots 395, 396, 403 and 404, from the Connecticut Land Company for the sum of $13,333.33.[22] These lots later became known as the Andrew Cozad (son of Samuel Cozad, Jr.) allotment. We will focus our attention on the portion of one-hundred acre lot, namely lot number 396, which was originally purchased by Mr. Cozad. It is on a portion of lot number 396 where the East Cleveland Township Cemetery is located.

The 1858 map of Cuyahoga County above, clearly documents lot 396 and the area that would become the cemetery with the initials "G.R.B." and that the size of the area was 14.62 acres. The initials "G.R.B." stands for Gay R. Beckwith. The next map in the timeline is the *1874 Atlas of Cuyahoga County* published by Titus, Simmons & Titus. This map clearly documents the existence of the cemetery.

The cemetery property was purchased on May 9, 1859 by the Trustees of East Cleveland Township from Edwin and Mariah Fuller, with the deed being recorded with the Cuyahoga County Recorder's

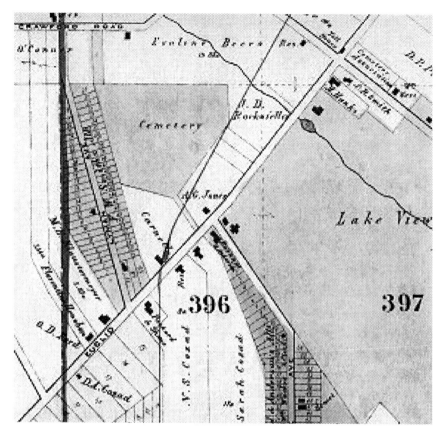

1874 Atlas of Cuyahoga County, Titus, Simmons & Titus

office on September 5, 1859, in Volume 102, Page 333. The deed reads as follows:

> *To all people to whom these presents shall come. Greetings: Know ye that we Edwin Fuller and Mariah his wife of East Cleveland Township, Cuyahoga County and State of Ohio for the consideration of Two thousand dollars, received to our full satisfaction of Daniel Adams, Frederick P. Sillsbee and A. Tolbert, Trustees of said Township and their successors in office, do give, grant, bargain, sell, and convey unto them the said Adams, Sillsbee and Tolbert, the following described tract of lot land situated in the Town of East Cleveland, in the County of Cuyahoga and State of Ohio, and is known as being a part of lot No. 396, in said Township;*

Beginning in the center of the Plank Road at a stone at the South West corner of Colmore's land. Hence South 43 3/4 , West 77 links to a stone, then 36° West 5 chains and 3 links to a stone.23 Thence North 75°, West 5 chains, 21 links to a stone. Thence North 12 1/2° West 9 chains 55 links on A Cozad's land to a stone on the South line of O. Connors land, on the old line. Thence South 89 1/2° East 12 chains 95 links to a stone on the North line of said lot 396 and at the N.W. corner of Samuel Cozad's land. Thence South 1/2°, East 360 links to a stone on Colmore's East line. Thence North 51 3/4° W 171 links to a stone in the swamp of Colmore's N.E. Corner. Thence South 27° West 8 chains 53 links to a stone at Colmore's N.W. corner. Thence South 36° East 4 chains 89 links to the place of beginning. Containing Ten acres it being purchased by said Trustees for a cemetery for the Township of East Cleveland, be the same more or less but subject to all legal highways. To have and to hold the above granted and bargained premises with the appurtenances thereunto belonging unto them the said Adams, Sillsbee and Tolbert and their successors in office and assigns forever, to their own proper use and behoof. And we the said Edwin Fuller and Mariah, do for ourselves and our heirs, executors and administrators covenant with the said Adams, Sillsbee and Tolbert and their successors that at and until the ensealing of these presents we were well seized of the premises as a good and indefeasible estate in fee simple and have good right to bargain and sell the same in manner and form as above written, and that the same be free from all encumbrance whatsoever. And furthermore we the said Edwin Fuller and Mariah do by these presents bind ourselves and our heirs forever, to warrant and depend the above granted and bargained premises to them, the said Adams, Sillsbee and Tolbert and their successors all my right and title dower in the above described premises. In witness whereof we have hereunto set our hands and seals the seventh day of May in the year of our Lord one thousand eight hundred and fifty nine.

Note should be made that the land that was originally East Cleveland Township Cemetery represented only 10 acres of land. One question that also arises and will remain unanswered is whether or not George Watkins, who according to the 1850 census was a resident of East Cleveland was a motivating force in the creation of the East Cleveland Township Cemetery.

We can now work back in time to determine ownership of the property. A drawing (Figure 4) has been made of the property, to assist in visualization of the property changes.

1. Edwin and Mariah Fuller purchased the property from Lasell and Rebecca A. Birge on January 7, 1857, with the deed being filed on February 28, 1857 and recorded in Volume 88, page 143. Gay R. Beckwith held a mortgage on the property from Edwin Fuller. The mortgage was executed on February 6, 1857 and recorded on February 23, 1857, in Volume 90, page 350. The mortgage is unreadable. The Cuyahoga County Recorders' office made every effort to find the original mortgage and/or a readable copy. The land in the original purchase is outlined in the drawing with a long dash and then a short dash.

2. Lasell Birge purchased the property from Thomas and Emily Phillips on October 30, 1854, with the deed being recorded on December 18, 1856 in Volume 85, page 621. It is labeled A in the drawing.

3. Benjamin Jones purchased from Andrew Cozad on July 18, 1836 the land labeled B in the drawing, with the deed recorded in Volume 21, page 497. Benjamin Jones sold this property to Emily Phillips on February 16, 1837, the deed was recorded on March 9, 1837 in Volume 22, page 84.

4. Thomas Phillips purchased from Andrew Cozad on April 27, 1842 the land labeled C in the drawing, the deed was recorded in Volume 31, page 578.

5. Silas Cozad heirs sold the property labeled D in the drawing to Thomas Phillips on April 28, 1854, the deed was recorded in Volume 91, page 95.

6. Samuel Cozad, Jr. purchased the property from the Connecticut Land Company on June 28, 1802.

An additional one acre of property was added to the cemetery on January 3, 1882. The Trustees of East Cleveland Township purchased the property from William B. and Sarah Howard for $1.00 (labeled E in the drawing), deed recorded in Volume 342, page 188.

Later several parcels of the original land were sold to the New York, Chicago and St. Louis Railway Company, as follows:

1. The parcel labeled F in the drawing was sold to the New York, Chicago and St. Louis Railway Company on December 2, 1882 for $1.00 and other consideration; deed recorded in Volume 348, page 450.

2. The parcel labeled G in the drawing was sold to the New York, Chicago and St. Louis Railway Company on May 26, 1909 by the Trustees of the Village of East Cleveland; deed recorded in Volume 1573, page 72. Due to annexation of a portion of East Cleveland to Cleveland Heights, a subsequent deed was executed by the Trustees of the City of Cleveland Heights for the same parcel of land on December 5, 1923; deed recorded Volume 2926, page 276.

The original entrance to the cemetery was on the North side of Euclid Avenue and was known as Cemetery Drive and was located nearly across the street from the current Euclid Avenue entrance to Lake View Cemetery. Immediately to the east of Cemetery Drive was property that was owned by Jeptha Wade. Rockefeller land also butted up against the back portion of the single lot section in the Northeast corner of the cemetery. Had the entrance remained on Euclid Avenue it is probable that the East Cleveland Township Cemetery would not have been lost to most Clevelanders for so many years.

When Cemetery Drive was sold to the railroad in 1909 the entrance was relocated to East 118th Street (formerly known as Lyman Street) this required several graves to be moved to allow for entry. The area affected

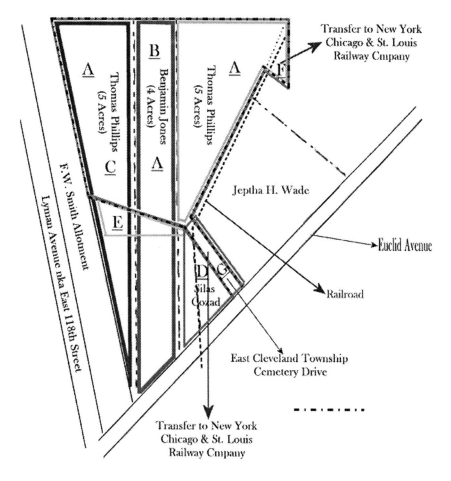

Figure 4 -- Author Drawing

by this new entrance was Section 10, with lots 110, 111 and 112 being eliminated. The lots purchased on East 118th Street were numbered 45 and 46 in F.W. Smith's Allotment.

At the site of the old entrance was a Tool Shed with Cemetery Drive extending to the main drive within the cemetery. Cemetery Drive ran between the southeast portion of sections 6 and 11 where they end at the southern portion of section 10. You can still see today the clearing where the tool shed stood and Cemetery Drive entered the cemetery.

When Cleveland Heights was created out of a portion of East Cleveland in 1901, both Cities assumed control over the cemetery. The cemetery was for a period of time referred to as the East Cleveland-Cleveland Heights Cemetery. The Trustees of the East Cleveland-Cleveland Heights Cemetery purchased lot number 45 on East 118th Street from William R. and Ellen Cozad Hopkins on June 4, 1909; the deed is recorded in Volume 1193, page 469. This lot is utilized as the current driveway into the cemetery. Mr. and Mrs. Hopkins sold the property to the Trustees with a restriction that the property only be utilized for a cemetery entrance or as a residential building.

The Trustees of the East Cleveland-Cleveland Heights Cemetery purchased lot number 46 on East 118th Street from William R. and Ellen Cozad Hopkins on June 7, 1910; the deed is recorded in Volume 1247, page 633. There is one building on the lot that is a combination cemetery office and chapel. Mr. and Mrs. Hopkins sold the property to the Trustees with a restriction that the property only be utilized for a cemetery entrance or as a residential building.

The Trustees of the East Cleveland and Cleveland Heights Cemetery purchased lot number 44 on East 118th Street from Stanley W. Jones on June 19, 1942; the deed is recorded in Volume 5449, page 133. On this lot was a two-story home that was used as the caretaker's home and subsequently rented.

The cemetery property is the same today as it was in 1892 when the property was annexed to the City of Cleveland with the exceptions noted above.

The Trustees of the East Cleveland Township Cemetery had to have contracted with a landscape architect to design the cemetery. With its triangular shape it would have been very easy for the cemetery to be designed in the customary square sections with rows as was the case with the Publick Burying Ground.

But it was 1859, and the pioneers in Cleveland were reaping the fruits of their labors over the past 60 years in the community. The residents were now more middle class citizens looking for a way to properly honor their ancestors in death. They wanted family plots they could own and where they could be placed to rest together. The City was also growing and becoming more of an urban area, rather than the rural areas that they were accustomed. The total population in Cuyahoga

County according to the 1860 census had increased to 78,033. Following the trend toward an appropriate final resting place, East Cleveland Township Cemetery was designed as a quasi-"garden" or "rural" style landscape architecture. Woodland Cemetery that was designed in 1853 had a similar design with irregularly shaped sections, but it would not be until the creation of Lake View Cemetery in 1869 that Cleveland would have it's first authentic garden style cemetery landscape design.

The design of the cemetery is very unique in that the sections are in various geometric designs with the lots within the sections outlining the design of the section. This is best visualized by inspecting the map of the cemetery below.

Despite the triangular shape of the land, the majority of the cemetery is designed in a circular pattern around the center of the cemetery

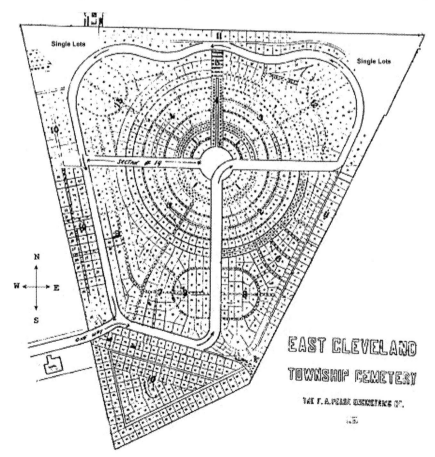

where the receiving vault was located. The main drive winds thru and around the grounds without conflicting with the patterns of the sections. Section 1 thru 5 creates the main circle around the center circle of the cemetery. Section 8 is an oblong circular design that actually crosses the drive. Sections 6, 9 and 11 create an internal scalloped border to the cemetery grounds. Section 13 offers a semi-circle in the center of this irregularly shaped section. Most of the cemetery was designed for family lots. There are only two areas that were originally designated for single graves. Graves in several of the family lots were later sold as single graves. The family lot was part of the design of the garden cemetery landscape design. During this time period whole families were buried on a family lot that would be the final resting place for anywhere from six to eight family members depending on the size of the lot. The family would visit the deceased, bring a picnic lunch and spend the day with the departed family members.

The first family lots purchased in the Cemetery were by John Doane (son of Timothy Doane) on April 3, 1859. The purchase was of lots 10, 11, 25 and 26 in Section 6. Mr. Doane paid $12 for all four lots for an average cost per lot of $3 each. The next lot recorded sold was not until September 6, 1859. By 1870 the average cost of a family lot had risen to $20. Thereafter, by 1900 the lot cost was varying based on the size of the lot with an average cost of approximately $50. Deeds were issued to the lot owners, a number of copies of the deeds were located, a sample is shown in Figure 5.

By the late 1960's, as the cemetery filled and revenues from lot sales decreased, Section 14 was added. Section 14 was created from what was part of the drive that went off the main drive to the North where the main drive intersected with the center circle. The burials in Section 14 occurred from 1970 onward.

Other than the changes noted above, the cemetery is in the same design and layout as it was in 1859. This is confirmed by the number of people transferred into the cemetery from 1859 to the mid-1860s that are buried in Sections 1 thru 6.

The cemetery today is a hidden park setting in the heart of University Circle. The railroad runs along the south side of the cemetery. You

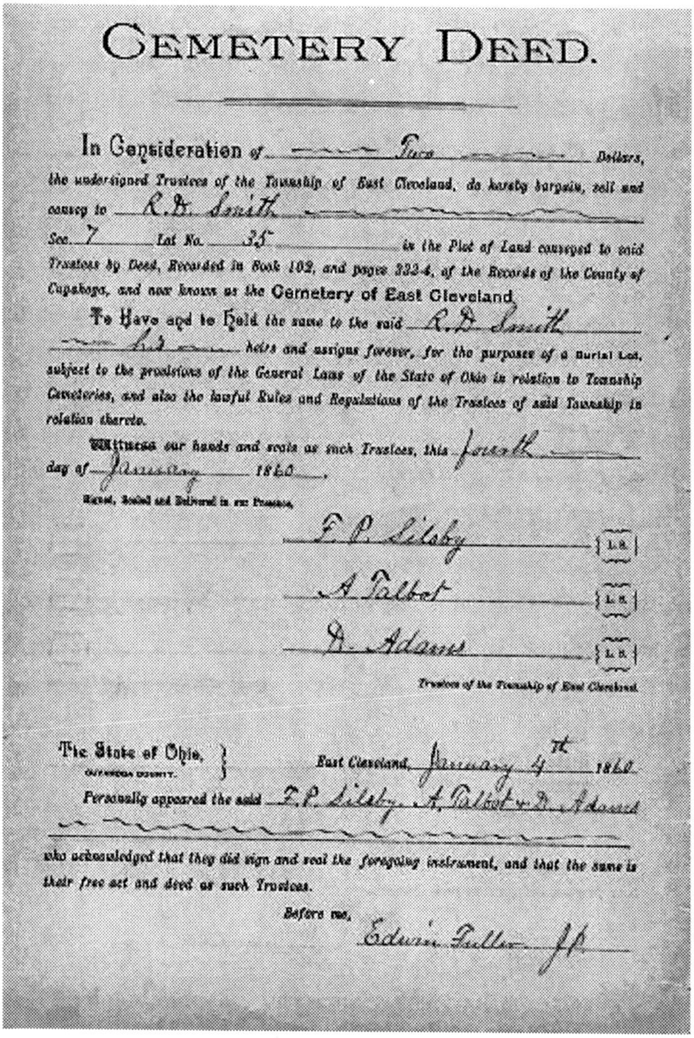

CEMETERY DEED.

In Consideration of ——— Two ——— Dollars, the undersigned Trustees of the Township of East Cleveland, do hereby bargain, sell and convey to R. D. Smith

Sec. 7 Lot No. 35 in the Plat of Land conveyed to said Trustees by Deed, Recorded in Book 102, and pages 332-4, of the Records of the County of Cuyahoga, and now known as the Cemetery of East Cleveland.

To Have and to Hold the same to the said R. D. Smith his heirs and assigns forever, for the purposes of a Burial Lot, subject to the provisions of the General Laws of the State of Ohio in relation to Township Cemeteries, and also the lawful Rules and Regulations of the Trustees of said Township in relation thereto.

Witness our hands and seals as such Trustees, this fourth day of January 1860.

Signed, Sealed and Delivered in our Presence,

F. P. Silsby {L.S.}

A. Talbot {L.S.}

D. Adams {L.S.}

Trustees of the Township of East Cleveland.

The State of Ohio, Cuyahoga County. } East Cleveland, January 4th 1860

Personally appeared the said F. P. Silsby, A. Talbot & D. Adams who acknowledged that they did sign and seal the foregoing instrument, and that the same is their free act and deed as such Trustees.

Before me, Edwin Fuller JP

Figure 5 - Author Photograph Collection

will hear the clickty-clack of the trains, as they travel on by. The grounds are scattered with a variety of mature trees that include weeping willows, sycamore, sweetgum, and spruce.

As you enter the cemetery you will pass through a wrought iron gate that was erected in approximately 1929 and see the flag pole with a marker at the base that was placed by the Memorial Day Association of Greater Cleveland remembering all veterans who "served, lived and died for their country". If you follow the gravel road around to your right you will see the Hudson, Norton and House monuments. By the time you get to the House monument you will start to curve your way back into the cemetery. By this point in your journey you may hear a train travel on by, but as you continue your journey you will be overcome by the quiet and peacefulness, despite the train. The headstones will call out to be read by the people that want to be remembered. You will be lost in the number of trees as you have now been transported out of the hustle and bustle of the City and all its concrete to a world that was started long ago.

Imagine all the things we do in a normal day in a circle, whether at home, school or work. With the cemetery designed in its circular pattern, one can get a visualization of the residents of the cemetery watching the road for each new arrival waiting to greet the new arrival as they begin their new journey. To take this visualization one step further imagine the residents in the circle sharing stories with each other regarding their lives and hearing about the changes that have occurred in the Western Reserve over a period of time that spans at least 200 years.

East Cleveland Township Cemetery ≈ Yesterday, Today & Tomorrow

Yesterday

You may be asking yourself: What and where was East Cleveland Township? In 1805 the township extended from East 9th Street (then known as Erie Street) to the Euclid Township line.[24] Picture no Euclid Avenue and when it was established being a dirt road known as Plank Road/Buffalo Road strewn with tree stumps. Imagine vast forests, with wild animals and Native American Indians being the majority of the inhabitants of the area. What we now know as the City of East Cleveland went through five major changes in boundaries to get where it is today.[25] East Cleveland Township was reorganized in 1846 with the boundaries being East 55th (formerly Willson Avenue) to the west and Windermere to the east. The City of Cleveland Heights was created from a portion of what was then East Cleveland; the City of Cleveland annexed another portion of the land in 1892 making Lakeview Road, East Cleveland's western boundary. East Cleveland has been known as a Township, Village, Hamlet and now a City. The East Cleveland Township ceased to exist as a legal entity in 1890 when it became the Hamlet of East Cleveland. The area that has been known as East Cleveland has changed size more times than any other city, township, hamlet, etc. in Cuyahoga County. Its boundaries can also claim to be the most irregularly shaped area in Cuyahoga County.

Mr. Duncan Headstone – Author Photograph Collection

From our earlier analysis of the land, we know that the property that became East Cleveland Township Cemetery was purchased on May 9, 1859, the deed was filed on August 31, 1859 (the date of the first burial of Mr. Duncan) and it was recorded by the Cuyahoga County Recorder's Office on September 5, 1859.

If there was a dedication ceremony for the cemetery, a record of the ceremony could not be located. None of the local newspapers reported on the creation of the cemetery. But exist it does.

The lack of a dedication ceremony may not have been an oversight. East Cleveland Township Cemetery is a multi-cultural cemetery. There are no racial, ethnic or religious lines drawn in the cemetery. There were many early cemeteries that were created under the philosophy that the land was blessed at the time of each burial according to the religious beliefs of the deceased.

There are indications that the cemetery was originally formed in 1850 or 1851.[26] It is believed that much like neighboring Woodland Cemetery, the decision was made in 1850 or 1851 to establish a cemetery; however, it took several years to obtain the funds to move forward with the project. What is known for certain is that the property purchased in 1859 was done under a law that allowed for townships to use general tax funds to establish and operate cemeteries. On January 31,

1892, Lot 396 (a portion of which contains East Cleveland Township Cemetery) was annexed to the City of Cleveland. S. J. Kelly writing for the *Cleveland Plain Dealer* relayed the following history: *"On Jan. 31, 1892, Cleveland stole a march on its neighbor by annexing Lots 404, 396, 388 and 387, and today the cities adjoin."*[27] The cemetery continued to be maintained by East Cleveland in its various stages until the Village of Cleveland Heights was created from a portion of East Cleveland in 1901. Thereafter, the two municipalities shared the care of the cemetery, and the cemetery became known as the East Cleveland – Cleveland Heights Cemetery. Despite annexation of the cemetery property located on Lot 396 to the City of Cleveland, Cleveland denied any responsibility for the cemetery.

When the entrance to the cemetery was moved from Euclid Avenue in approximately 1909, due to the sale of land to the Railroad, to East 118th Street, lot number 45 became the driveway/entrance and lot number 46 was utilized to create a cemetery office and chapel. On October 5, 1910 a building permit was obtained from the City of Cleveland (Permit Number 33615) to erect the structure that would become the office and chapel. The building was designed by well known architect, Frank B. Meade. The office/chapel was officially completed on December 27, 1910.

Frank B. Meade was one of the leading residential architects of Cleveland. He began his architectural career in the late 1800's and continued until 1941. Mr. Meade studied architecture at Massachusetts Institute of Technology and opened his own office in Cleveland in 1893. His goal was to specialize in homes for affluent Clevelanders, who during this period, were found on Euclid Avenue.[28]

Partnerships formed between Mr. Meade and other prominent Cleveland architects, namely, Alfred Granger, Abram Garfield (son of the United States President James A. Garfield), and James Hamilton. He lived on Euclid Avenue, was active in Cleveland's social circles, and was the founding president of the Hermit Club. As families migrated to the suburbs of Wade Park, Bratenahl, and Shaker Heights, Frank Meade was retained to design their homes; he also designed large residences for the Villages of Ambler Heights and Euclid Heights. It was during

East Cleveland Township Cemetery Chapel
Author Photograph Collection

the last 30 years of his career, with partner James Hamilton that his practice flourished.

You can see Mr. Meade's style found in the office/chapel in other of his works. The building was constructed from Norway Pine and brick. The walls and basement are all brick. The ceiling is vaulted with the roof being tiled. The arched windows on the front and sides correspond to the arched entrance that adds to the building's charm. The other homes located on East 118th Street surrounding the cemetery are all designed in a Victorian colonial style. The fact that the chapel is a Spanish colonial design catches your attention when traveling past the cemetery.

The chapel was utilized for funeral services, with the earliest record of a funeral being held on November 21, 1911 for Philena Higgins. The most recent record of a funeral being held in the chapel was in 1948, however, the office/chapel continued to be utilized by the caretakers of the cemetery through at least 1979. There were a number of funeral homes that assisted in the burials of our early settlers. Many of which are no longer in existence, yet a picture was located of a horse drawn hearse from Millard & Son. J.F. Millard was the original owner, he was born in approximately 1824 in Connecticut and was married to Lucretia

Wm. I. (Frank) Rich with Nellie of the Hearse Team
Taken in rear of J. F. Millard's Home – 1913
The Western Reserve Historical Society, Cleveland, Ohio

(nee Cattin). Millard & Son eventually became known as Millard Son & Raper Co.

Prior to the construction of the chapel, funeral services would normally be held in the home of the deceased and/or the home of a family member. The use of funeral homes for visitation and services was also becoming more common. Prior to this time the funeral homes would only supply the casket, horse drawn hearse from the family home to the cemetery, and coordinate the burial of the deceased.

The cemetery records document that East Cleveland Township Cemetery also acted as an agent to arrange for the deceased to be shipped to their homeland for burial. The records document the shipment of five Chinese individuals back to China for burial, they were: Chin On, died October 11, 1911; John Lee, died September 3, 1914; Sam Lee, died November 20, 1917; Harry Hong, died January 7, 1919; and Hong Yee, died January 5, 1931.

For many years up to 1929 the trustees of the cemetery consisted of John Cannon, an attorney who was instrumental in the development

Cleveland Memory Project, Cleveland State University

of the Terminal Tower; and Frederick King. The trustee positions were filled by the East Cleveland Commission and Cleveland Heights Council. When Mr. Cannon passed away in 1929 there was a trustee vacancy. The trustees appointed were Ben Wickham by Cleveland Heights council; Frederick King continued as the East Cleveland representative; and E.B. Merrell who was vice president of the Cleveland Trust Company was added as a third trustee.

It was also in 1929 that the railroad erected the retaining wall that still exists today. It was because of this construction project that pictures were found of the cemetery at that time.

The photograph above, off to your left you will see the old tool shed which is also where the original entrance to the cemetery was located. What was left at this time of the original drive runs from the tool shed up to the main road.

Cleveland Memory Project, Cleveland State University

The photograph above, documents the center of the cemetery where the receiving vault was located. Receiving vaults were an important structure for the early cemeteries. The receiving vault was the building where the deceased were brought until the burial could be completed. During winter months in Cleveland when the ground was frozen the deceased would be placed in the receiving vault until the grave could be dug. At this point in time graves were dug by hand.

The headstones in the picture clearly document the circular direction of the lots. This is the only picture that could be found of the receiving vault. In a blow-up of this picture, you can see the intricate detail of the receiving vault. The masonry work around the arched door and the circular window above the door were beautiful.

Around 1929 the trustees began questioning their legal rights to govern the cemetery since East Cleveland Township no longer existed and was the legal owner of the property. A request was made for the State of Ohio Auditors to review the matter. It is believed that the first audit conducted by the State of Ohio Auditors was completed for the

Cleveland Memory Project, Cleveland State University

period ending December 31, 1929. A copy of this report is missing from the cemetery records, with the State of Ohio Auditors office indicating the records no longer exist within their office archives. However, the report is mentioned in each of the subsequent audit reports that were completed by State of Ohio Auditors. The auditors found that the governance of the cemetery was questionable, yet no solutions to the situation were put forth.

On March 26, 1930 a meeting was held between Alfred Clum, assistant Cleveland law director, George Hartshorn, solicitor of Cleveland Heights and E.A. Binyon, solicitor of East Cleveland to attempt to determine ownership of the cemetery land then valued at approximately $100,000 and cemetery funds that had accumulated to approximately the same level.[29] This meeting produced no resolution to the on-going question of ownership, thus, responsibility for the cemetery.

On May 27, 1930 instructions from Trustee Ben Wickham regarding the care and maintenance of the cemetery were sent to Cemetery Superintendent William E. Jones. The letter contains some interesting facts that seem to indicate that the cemetery may have started its decline prior to this time but there was a movement to get the maintenance back on track and is cited below:

An inspection of the cemetery by Trustees has resulted in my authority to give to you the following instructions:

1. *You will at once cause the interior of the chapel to be redecorated with a color somewhat lighter than that now existing on the walls and to have the interior wood work revarnished. Prior to this you will have the fire-place in the chapel room bricked up and the bricks plastered over so that the space now occupied by the brickworking and around the fire-place will present a smooth appearance. This not only applies to the chapel proper but to all rooms in the chapel building.*

2. *You will see that the interior of this chapel is kept absolutely clean and the furnishings in first class condition.*

3. *You will keep the chapel room locked at all times when same is not used but the toilet rooms are to be left open for use of those visiting the cemetery and, if necessary, separate entrance be provided for the ladies toilet.*

4. *You will provide a location on some ground now under cemetery control for the burial of the three bodies in the vault; one of which, we understand, has remained there fifteen years, one for ten years and one for one year.*

5. *You will cause to be cleaned up and carted away all rubbish and refuse in the rear of the vault and will keep this spot clean and free from rubbish hereafter.*

6. *You will cause to be installed at proper places around the cemetery wire containers for reception of refuse and see that these are regularly emptied. You will employ men and teams with proper implements to level off the drives in the cemetery where the same are rutted and uneven. You will see that all grass or weeds are cut down where the same have been allowed to reach any height and keep the grass cut close along the edges of the drives and around the monuments. In order to accomplish all these specific needs, you will employ such help as is not now sufficient and you can employ other temporary help as is necessary to bring this cemetery to order and neatness as perfect as can reasonably be obtained.*

We propose to build a new fence, as you know, on the west and south lines and to build a line of ornamental fence and ornamental gates across the open space at the entrance in line with the existing fence. We are contracting with the Cylcone Fence Co. to build this ornamental fence and gates. You are authorized to buy the proper material and obtain labor to build stone posts either side of the drive under direction of the company erecting such fence and gates.

After the erection of such fence and gates, you will establish regular hours for opening and closing these gates so that these gates will be closed and locked during the night season.

Generally you are instructed to use your best efforts to keep this cemetery in absolutely as neat and trim a condition as is possible and you will be held accountable for its being kept in such condition. The Trustees, individually, will make inspection of the cemetery to see that these instructions are being carried out.[30]

In 1938, Garland Ashcraft, reporter for the *Cleveland Press* wrote that the *"City's Orphan Cemetery Prospers Without Owner."*[31] The issue of ownership was still being debated in a 1960 *Cleveland Plain Dealer* article entitled *"E. Cleveland Foster Mom to Cemetery."*[32] According to this article it is indicated that the City of East Cleveland was operating the *"orphaned cemetery"* with *"some moral support from Cleveland Heights."* Even though State of Ohio auditors had questioned the legality of the board, no workable alternative had been found.

In a July 24, 1941 letter to the City of Cleveland Heights, the State of Ohio Auditor's office indicated that in the case of *King v. City of Shelby, 40 O. App. 195,* the court found that a township could deed cemetery property to a city at the time of annexation of the property where a cemetery is located. Upon reviewing the annexation file that included lot 396 to the City of Cleveland, there was no specific reference to the cemetery. The issue of ownership of the cemetery continued and the cemetery's decline continued.

In the *Cleveland Plain Dealer* on July, 3, 1988, Brent Larkin put forth his commentary regarding the condition of the cemetery, as previously cited in the Introduction. The *Call and Post* raised questions regarding the cemetery in 1994 when reporter Armetta Landrum indicated the cemetery *"looks like something straight out of a horror series."*[33]

In 1998 the debates regarding the cemetery came to a head when the City of Cleveland filed suit against the Cities of East Cleveland and Cleveland Heights in Cleveland Municipal Court, Housing Division bearing case numbers 98-CRB-33609 and 98-CRB-33610. Cleveland claimed that despite the fact the property was and had been located in the City of Cleveland since 1892, the Cities of East Cleveland and Cleveland Heights were responsible for the dilapidated condition of the cemetery and the two adjacent houses, which it indicated was criminal neglect.[34] Motions to Dismiss the action filed by Cleveland were submitted to Judge Raymond L. Pianka by the Cities of East Cleveland and Cleveland Heights. In the Motions to Dismiss the Cities claimed they were not the *"owners"* of the cemetery property. Judge Pianka denied the Motion to Dismiss based on the control documented over the years by the Cities of East Cleveland and Cleveland Heights of the cemetery property.

Another law suit was filed in Cuyahoga County Common Pleas court on November 9, 1998 by the Cities of Cleveland Heights and East Cleveland against the City of Cleveland, KeyBank, Selena Clark and Xavier Roldan. In this law suit, the two cities asked the Court to find that the City of Cleveland was the *"owner"* of the cemetery property based on Ohio Revised Code Section 759.08 that states:

> *The title to and right of possession of public cemeteries and burial grounds located within a municipal corporation and set apart and dedicated as public cemeteries or burials grounds, and grounds used as such by the public but not dedicated, except those owned or under the care of a religious or benevolent society, or an incorporated company or associated, are hereby vested in the municipal corporation in which such cemetery or burial ground is located.*

The lawsuit also indicated that Selena Clark and Xavier Roldan may have ownership of the property located at 1621 and 1615 East 118th Street as they had taken up residence in the buildings at these locations.

The ownership of the East Cleveland Township Cemetery continued to be debated in the courts. In February, 2001 the East Cleveland Township Cemetery Foundation was incorporated under Chapter 1702 of the Ohio Revised Code, in the State of Ohio. The incorporators were Allen H. Ford, William L. Garrison and Roy G. (Dutch) Harley. East Cleveland Township Cemetery Foundation became a party in Cuyahoga County Common Pleas Court case number 369386. In June, 2003 a settlement agreement was reached between all parties involved in said case wherein ownership in the property associated with East Cleveland Township Cemetery was transferred to the Foundation. As part of the settlement agreement, the Cities of Cleveland, Cleveland Heights and East Cleveland agreed to continue to assist in maintenance of the cemetery for five years from the date of the settlement or until such time as the Foundation raised $1 million.

As in the case of the Publick Burying Ground the debate over ownership of the land came to an end. The only difference is that the East Cleveland Township Cemetery continues to exist. Thus, after nearly 75 years of debate, East Cleveland Township Cemetery is no longer orphaned. It has a legal owner and one can only hope that the East Cleveland Township Cemetery Foundation will create a legacy that will properly represent the dignity and respect due to the residents of its cemetery. And as was the case in Dickens' case of *Jarndyce and Jarndyce* referred to in relationship to the Publick Burying Ground, the only appropriate answer to the question of whether the issue of ownership for East Cleveland Township Cemetery is finally settled would be *"probably."*

Today

East Cleveland Township Cemetery Foundation was created through the vision of William L. Garrison its President. Mr. Garrison joined Lake View Cemetery in 1985 as its President and became aware of East Cleveland Township Cemetery due to its close proximity to Lake View Cemetery. East Cleveland Township Cemetery and Lake View Cemetery are located nearly across Euclid Avenue from each other.

In the mid 1980's Mr. Garrison was approached by David K. Ford asking that someone look into properly caring for East Cleveland Township Cemetery or he was considering moving his ancestors that are buried in East Cleveland Township Cemetery to Lake View Cemetery. Lake View Cemetery had no relationship to East Cleveland Township Cemetery other than they were both tied in different ways to the Cities of Cleveland, Cleveland Heights and East Cleveland. Murray M. Davidson who was with University Circle, Inc. also approached Mr. Garrison during this time period and suggested Lake View Cemetery assume responsibility for East Cleveland Township Cemetery, suggesting that it consider buying the residential lots surrounding the cemetery as a possible way to expand and revitalize the cemetery.

Mr. Garrison met with Cities of East Cleveland and Cleveland Heights to determine the current status and legal implications of Lake View Cemetery assuming ownership of the cemetery. The endowment that East Cleveland Township Cemetery had at one point of approximately $250,000 was now nearly non-existent.. Lake View Cemetery explored the possibility of assuming responsibility for East Cleveland

Township Cemetery, however, the Trustees of Lake View Cemetery decided it was not in the best interest of Lake View Cemetery nor was it in its long term goals to assume responsibility for East Cleveland Township Cemetery.

Mr. Garrison continued to be interested in East Cleveland Township Cemetery and in fact his son completed a Boy Scout project at the cemetery. In approximately 1998 when the previously discussed law suits were pending between the Cities of Cleveland, Cleveland Heights and East Cleveland, Mr. Garrison was approached by the City of Cleveland to determine if Lake View Cemetery would be willing to assume responsibility for East Cleveland Township Cemetery. That question already having been addressed by the Trustees at Lake View Cemetery, Mr. Garrison suggested that he would be willing to explore establishing a separate Foundation for East Cleveland Township Cemetery that would create an endowment and care for the cemetery.

William J. Culbertson, an attorney at Squire, Sanders & Dempsey was assigned to assisting in establishing the East Cleveland Township Cemetery Foundation as a tax exempt 501(c)3 corporation. It took several attempts at the tax exempt status as their was no prior model that Mr. Culbertson could find in which to create a Foundation for a cemetery that was in fact a charitable trust.

Mr. Garrison approached Allen H. Ford and Roy G. (Dutch) Harley to be founding members of the Foundation. Mr. Ford was asked because of his family ties to the cemetery but also because he brought to the Foundation a great analytical business sense. Mr. Ford was also a past member of the Lake View Cemetery Board. Mr. Harley is a resident of the City of East Cleveland and had worked with Mr. Garrison on several other projects including Forest Hills Park in East Cleveland. Mr. Harley has a background in construction, one previous position being as past President of Albert Higley Company, that would be beneficial to the Foundation as renovation plans for the cemetery began to develop.

Once the Foundation obtained ownership of the cemetery in June 2003 additional Trustees were added and today the Board includes: William L. Garrison, President; Allen H. Ford, Vice President and Secretary; Nancy L. West, Vice President and Assistant Secretary; Roy

G. (Dutch) Harley, Vice President and Treasurer; Michelle A. Day, Vice President and Assistant Treasurer; William J. Culbertson, Murray M. Davidson, Kathleen H. Lambacher, Bracy E. Lewis , and J. Wayne Rhine as Trustees.

When asked why the interest in a long forgotten cemetery, Mr. Garrison replied "Just my altruistic need to give back to the community what it has provided to me and to allow those families who placed the care of their deceased relatives in the care of the East Cleveland Township Cemetery to have peace that those relatives are being properly looked after."

The renovations of the cemetery started to take shape in the fall of 2004 with Michelle A. Day and Nancy L. West leading the charge. Renovations began in January 2005 of the burial chapel with J. Wayne Rhine and his family also joining the efforts in early 2005. Grounds maintenance was started by the Trustees and a group of community volunteers in 2004 and 2005 was augmented when the Foundation became an agency for Court Community Service. In March, 2005 Bob Deskins, owner of Lightning Demolition and Excavating stepped forward and volunteered to demolish the former caretakers home that was beyond repair. He was followed by Davy Tree and Ardmore Tree Services who stepped forward and provided the Foundation with assistance in caring for all the trees in the cemetery.

Absolute Roofing donated the use of scaffolding indefinetly to the Foundation for its use in refinishing the ceiling and wood beams within the chapel. Nathaniel Hein, a Boy Scout working on his Eagle Scout project came forward and started the project of stripping the chapel's wood beams of white paint.

Sunken headstones are being raised, monuments toppled by age and weather are being put right. Safety and security renovations were completed in 2006 due to funding by The Abington Foundation that included replacement of the chain link fence, renovation and restoration of the cast iron front gate, repairs to the three mausoleums and the purchase of a shed for the storage of grounds maintenance tools.

When reports of the demolition of the caretaker's home in March 2005 made the newspaper, the Foundation was contacted by Merry Cerwin, the daughter of former caretaker Harold Romanis. Ms. Cerwin now comes to the cemetery and assists the other volunteers on taking care of the cemetery and caring on the legacy her father inspired in her as a child.

On the vacant lot where the caretaker's home was located, the Men's Garden Club of Greater Cleveland offered landscape design services of Ronald Hartmiller to the Foundation to design a community sculpture garden. Neighborhood Connections, a small grant program through the Cleveland Foundation has provided the Foundation with two grants to fund the infrastructure for the garden. As part of this process the cemetery property was surveyed for the first time since 1859.

East Cleveland Township Cemetery Foundation also established an endowment fund with the Cleveland Foundation in 2006.

Harold Romanis with Grounds Crew
East Cleveland Township Cemetery
Merry Cerwin Photograph Collection

Tomorrow

What does tomorrow hold for East Cleveland Township Cemetery? The future is looking bright for the cemetery. It held its first Memorial Day Ceremony in decades in 2006 followed in July by a documentary on the renovations taking place at the cemetery by Rick Jackson at WVIZ. The families of the permanent residents of the cemetery are coming back to visit in droves and are helping to support the cemetery in reaching it mission and vision of:

Mission Statement

The mission of the East Cleveland Township Cemetery Foundation is to own and maintain the East Cleveland Township Cemetery as a historic landmark, to restore, preserve and share the cemetery's pioneer Victorian heritage and to build a solid financial foundation for the cemetery's future.

Vision Statement

As one of the few and possibly the only public charity to own, renovate and maintain an abandoned historic pioneer cemetery and to relieve the previous public owners of their need to use public resources critically needed for the general welfare of its people, the East Cleveland Township Cemetery Foundation will strive to set an exemplary example of community leadership and responsibility to turn a community blight into a community light.

There is still much to be done, however, the East Cleveland Township Cemetery Foundation Trustees and all its volunteers are committed to making certain the early families of Cleveland are not forgotten again.

The Three Mausoleums

East Cleveland Township Cemetery has three mausoleums. Information regarding the people in these final resting places is limited. Yet, it would seem appropriate that we discuss these families.

Benjamin J. Gray came to Cleveland from England where he was born in 1830. Buried with him in the mausoleum located in Section 13, are Hanna Gray born in 1826 and passed away on September 10, 1907 along with Margaret Gray, born in 1826 and passed away in 1888. The lot for the mausoleum was purchased on October 25, 1890.

Gray Mausoleum – Author Photograph Collection

Mr. Gray served in the Civil War, having enlisted as a Private on August 24, 1861, in Company K, 2nd Cavalry Regiment Ohio on October 10, 1861. He received a disability discharge from Company K, 2nd Cavalry Regiment Ohio on May 12, 1862

According to the 1880 census Benjamin and Marguerite Gray were living in East Cleveland. Mr. Gray was working as a gardener.

Hale Mausoleum – Author Photograph Collection

Jonathan Hale was born in Massachusetts in 1807. Mr. Hale and his wife Harriett, born in New York, are believed to have been living in Ohio by at least 1842 when their oldest child, Mary was born. According to the 1860 census they were living in Euclid. The children were as follows: Mary, age 18; Rosa, Edward, age 12; George W., age 10; Rosa, age 7; Darwin, age 6; Andrew J., age 11/12. By the 1880 census there were two additional children, Nellie, age 15; and Otis age 10. Mr. Hale's occupation is listed as farmer.

According to the burial records, Jonathan and Harriet along with their son Edward are resting in the Hale Mausoleum located in Section 5. It was not documented in the records when the lot for this mausoleum was purchased.

Nearby is son, Darwin and his wife Lucy in Section 3, Lot 44. Also in this lot are Florence, Pearl, and Arthur D. children of Darwin and Lucy.

Moses Mausoleum – J. Wayne Rhine Photograph Collection

C. Elihu Moses and his wife Elizabeth (nee Talbot) were married in Farmington, Connecticut on April 22, 1798 at the New Haven Second Church.[35] According to the records found they had settled in Ohio by 1804[36]. Children born to C. Elihu and Elizabeth were Ardolissa, born in 1799; Charles, born in 1800; Elihu, born in 1806; Philo P., born in 1809; Luther, born in 1811; and Roxana, born in 1813. C. Elihu was the son of Othniel Moses who was a veteran of the Revolutionary War.

C. Elihu served as a captain under Colonel John S. Edward's Regiment, Ohio Militia in the War of 1812 from August 24, 1812 to September 5, 1812. He was discharged on September 3, 1812 by General Elijah Wadsworth. He rejoined his company in Detroit on September 3, 1814 which was no under the command of his Lieutenant Hezekiah Hine. The military muster roll reports that he was sick for the period of September 3, 1814 to November 30, 1814. Later records indicate he died in Cleveland on December 10, 1814 and was originally buried on Public Square.

The War of 1812 is considered one of the forgotten wars. merica stunned the world when it declared war on Great Britain. He United States wanted Great Britain out of North American, specifically Canada. The war ended after 2 years much as it began, however, the American maintained control of Baltimore and New Orleans. Several naval battles demonstrated to Great Britain that it was superior to similarly sized British vessels. It was also the War of 1812 that gave us the saying *"Don't give up the ship"* when in 1813 Captain James Lawrence shouted it to his crew just before his death.

Elizabeth Talbot Moses passed away in 1839. The lot ownership records indicate that C. Elihu and Elizabeth's son Luther purchased the lots where the mausoleum stands on July 23, 1873. The mausoleum has the year of 1879 which would appear to indicate this was the year it was constructed. The lots were later sold to C. Elihu and Elizabeth's son-in-law, A. H. Avery who was married to their daughter Ardolissa.

Ardolissa and A. H. Avery along with other members of the Avery family are buried around the mausoleum in Section 12, Lots 15 and 16.

C. Elihu and Elizabeth's son Elihu and his wife Ann are buried off to the right and behind the mausoleum in Section 12, Lot 28.

The mausoleum is in serious need of repairs and has been the subject of articles written regarding the cemetery for years. This past summer an effort was made to clean out the debris that had accumulated in the mausoleum after the roof gave way, plans are now underway to renovate the mausoleum and the Moses monument immediately to the right of the mausoleum.

Elizabeth Talbot Moses was said have been a descendant of Lord John Talbot of England. It is believed that Elizabeth Talbot Moses was an aunt of John T. Talbot buried in Section 2, Lot 17. John T. Talbot's daughter Margaret Eliza married Horace Ford. Margaret Eliza (nee Talbot) Ford became a member of the Daughters of the American Revolution based on her relationship with Othniel Moses.[37]

Margaret Eliza Talbot Ford resides on the Talbot family plot which is next to the Ford family plot. Her funeral was held in the cemetery's chapel on March 26, 1920.

Our Heroes and Tragedies

Every town and city in America has its heroes, tragedies and collection of memories. Each cemetery likewise can tell the stories of heroes and recount the tragedies of the town or city in which it was established. In this section we will remember some of our heroes and tragedies that affected our community and the residents of the cemetery.

Since the beginning of this country we have had our heroes, many of which defended this country and the beliefs which are the foundation of our freedoms. East Cleveland Township Cemetery is the final resting place for at least 430 veterans of all the major conflicts this nation has faced starting with the American Revolution through the war in Vietnam. Since September 11, 2001 we have redefined our definition of heroes to also include the police and firemen who protect us on a day-to-day basis. A list of the men and woman who served this country from the American Revolution to the War in Vietnam and who are buried in the cemetery are listed in Table 7.

Civil War Heroes

Alonzo Silsby was born in Warrensville Heights, Ohio on October 18, 1839 the son of Alfred and Clarissa (nee Carter) Silsby. On August 29, 1862 he enlisted in the Army and was assigned to Company Battery I, 1st Light Artillery Regiment Ohio during the Civil War.

On July 1st, 2nd and 3rd of 1863 the Battle of Gettysburg was taking place between General Robert E. Lee's Army of 75,000 men and Union Army of the Potomac (97,000 men) under General George G. Meade.

This major battle did not end the Civil War, however it is reported that more men fought and more men died than in any other battle.

One of the casualties was the subject of this biographical sketch. Mr. Silsby was wounded on July 2, 1863 and subsequently died of the wounds he received. He is buried in Section 3, Lot 33.

Charles Dille was born March 11, 1820 in Euclid, Ohio the son of Asa and Polly Dille. On September 1, 1862 at the age of 42 he enlisted in the Army. He served as a private in Company I, Regiment 23 of the Ohio Infantry. On May 9, 1864 Mr. Dille was captured by Confederates at Cloyd's Mountain in West Virginia. He was taken to Andersonville Prison in Georgia. The prison itself was 26-1/2 acres and was surrounded by a 15 foot high stockade of pine logs. Sentry boxes stood at 30 yard intervals along the top of the stockade. Nineteen feet from the stockade was a line or "Deadline" that the prisoners were forbidden to cross or face death. By June, 1864 there were at least 26,000 men confined in the prison that was intended to hold only 13,000.

The Confederate government began having difficulty maintaining adequate living conditions at the prison in the form of housing, food, clothing and medical care for its prisoners that created a great amount of suffering and a high mortality rate. A depiction of Andersonville Prison was made on July 2, 1864 and can be seen below.

Charles Dille died at Andersonville Prison during the Civil War, on July 22, 1864 due to starvation. He now rests in Section 6, Lot 6.

Alexander Swain was born in approximately 1843 in Harrison County, Ohio the son of Benjamin and Rebecca Swain. On July 4, 1863 he enlisted in the Army and was assigned to Company D, 3rd Regiment of the United States Colored Infantry during the Civil War which was commanded by Colonel Tillman. According to his military record he was taken prisoner on May 10, 1864 in Jacksonville Florida and subsequently transferred to Fort Marion in St. Augustine, Florida. He reported the conditions at Fort Marion as requiring him to lay in a damp cell with no ventilation. Mr. Swain was honorably discharged on October 31, 1865 in Philadelphia, Pennsylvania. He and his wife Ann (nee Ford) rests in Section 11, North Plot, Row 24, Grave 402.

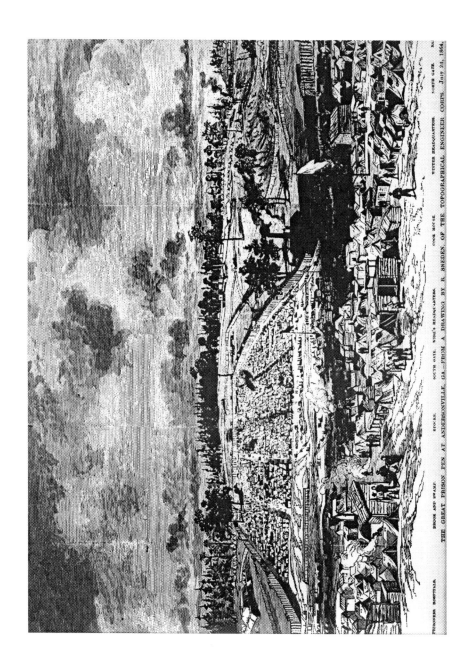

THE GREAT PRISON PEN AT ANDERSONVILLE, GA.—FROM A DRAWING BY R. SNEDEN, OF THE TOPOGRAPHICAL ENGINEER CORPS. JULY 23, 1864.

Captain John Grady --

As you travel the main road around the cemetery and look off to your left as you round the corner near the rear of the cemetery; the monument of Captain John Grady with his jacket, hat and ax draped over the top stands tall and proud.

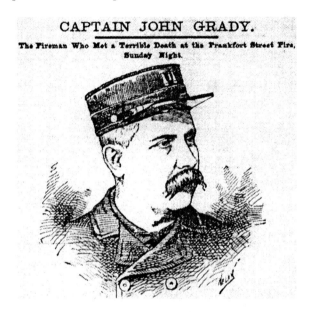

Cleveland Press, November 17, 1891

On November 16, 1891 the headline of the *Cleveland Plain Dealer* read *"Death's Flames, an Early Evening Fire and Its Disastrous Results. A Brave Fireman Killed, Two Hurt."* The fire began in the Short & Forman building which was a printing company facing Frankfort Street. The front portion of the burnt building was formerly a hotel known as the Franklin house, the first hotel erected in Cleveland.

The fire began shortly after 8:00 PM on November 15, 1891 and by 9:00 PM every piece of fire fighting equipment in the city has been called to the scene.

Even the fireboat was pumping a two-inch stream up Superior street from the river to the rear of William Bingham company's store. Within ten minutes after the alarm sounded the entire build-ing was enveloped in flames and the wonder of it is that the entire block, including the Weddell and Johnson houses, was not swept out of existence.[38]

The fire spread quickly from the first floor to the fourth floor of the building, and shot out the roof.

THE BIG FIRE OF SUNDAY NIGHT - A VIEW OF FRANKFORT ST. WEST FROM BANK.

Cleveland Press, November 16, 1891

Capt. Grady and Cadet Ward rushed into Tim Haley's saloon with a line of hose but were driven back by the smoke. They made a second attempt and had begun to play when the roof fell in. Its weight was too much for the remaining floors, already weakened by the flames, and the entire interior of the structure was precipi-tated upon the two brave firemen. Ward was pinned down under a pile of debris. A dozen brave men rushed to his rescue, directed by his agonizing cries. They quickly released him and carried his bruised and mangled form to the fire station on St. Clair street.

Capt. Grady had unfortunately penetrated deeper into the build-
ing than Ward and a large pile of debris stood between him and
life. A desperate effort was made to tear the wreckage aside, but it
was unsuccessful.

A half hour later the entire structure collapsed into Frankfort street
crushing Hook and Ladder truck number 2 to the ground under the
weight of the falling walls.

The search for Captain Grady was delayed due to the heat and
smoke. The following morning, Captain Grady's father, Patrick Grady,
stood waiting anxiously watching the search for the body of his son.
At home, Captain Grady's wife and three small children had heard the
devastating news the night before. By 1:30 in the afternoon, half of the
debris had been cleared from Haley's saloon and still there was no trace
of Captain Grady. The firemen were being assisted by City workers and
employees of the Gas Company. When evening descended, the search
was given up, with plans to resume the following morning.[39]

The search resumed the following day with additional workers hired
by Captain Grady's brother, Michael. Mayor Rose also arranged for the
entire City street department to be assigned to assist in the search for
Captain Grady.

Cleveland Press, November 17, 1891

It was Captain Grady's brother-in-law, William Pickering, who located the Captain's remains shortly after 2:00 PM on Tuesday, November 17. A dozen men assisted in removing the debris that buried Captain Grady and it took all these men to remove Captain Grady's remains from what still remained of the building.

Captain Grady's funeral was held on Friday, November 20, 1891 from his home at 31 Booker Avenue. He was remembered as follows:

> *In life Capt. Grady was known in a limited circle as a brave fireman and an upright man; in heroic death he was known to every man, woman and child in Cleveland and he was worthy of the remarkable tribute paid to him at the funeral services yesterday afternoon.*[40]

The Cleveland Press summarized his service as a fireman in the City of Cleveland:

> *Captain John Grady of engine company No. 1, who met a terrible death in the Short & Forman fire, Sunday night, was one of the best fire fighters in the Cleveland department. He had charge of a company stationed in the very heart of the city, and which has been considered one of the most important in the service. He entered the department in 1881, was promoted to lieutenant, Oct. 24, 1884, and captain, Jan. 31, 1889. Captain Grady was a popular fireman, his ability and genial good nature making him friends both personally and in his line of duty. He leaves a wife and three children at 31 Broker av. He was about 35 years old.*[41]

Captain Grady was born in Ireland. He and his family left Ireland during the potato famine bound for the United States to begin their new lives. He married Susannah Pickering and had four children at the time of his death, Maud, born in 1884; John E., born in 1886; Albert, born in 1889 and passed away in January, 1890; and Gertrude born in 1890. As of this writing one of Captain Grady's granddaughters still resides in Cleveland. It was a pleasure to speak with her and her niece.

Susannah never remarried and raised the children alone. She owned and operated a restaurant in Cleveland for many years, prior to her retirement. They reside in Section 12, Lot 67.

The 1895 Central Viaduct Tragedy

The Central Viaduct no longer exists in Cleveland after having been closed in 1941 and demolished during World War ll. However, on Saturday, November 16, 1895 when Edward Hoffman headed off to work as conductor of Car 642 for Cleveland Electric Railway, the Central Viaduct was part of the normal route for Car 642. It was also a normal busy Saturday with many Clevelanders out shopping or visiting with relatives.[42]

The viaduct was a drawbridge over the Cuyahoga River, and it was not uncommon to have to wait for the bridge to open and close for river traffic. There was a safety switch located approximately 225 feet from the drawbridge that when working properly diverted traffic off the main track to rails leading to the side of the viaduct. On this day at approximately 7:00 PM the safety mechanisms that were installed to notify traffic to stop for the opening and closing of the draw failed.

Central Viaduct, Cleveland, Ohio

Author Postcard Collection

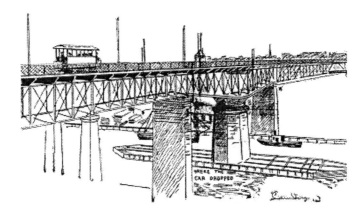

Cleveland Press

Cleveland Press

Car 642 and its 20 to 25 passengers tumbled off the bridge and into the river to their death in the Cuyahoga River.

Edward Hoffman, the conductor of Car 642 was born in Germany and was 23 years old when he died as a result of this horrible accident that was recorded by the *Cleveland Press* as "*Nothing like it has been recorded in the History of the Forest City.*" He was married with a 10 month old son, named Freddie at the time of his death. The Coroner's File Number 3313 documents that Mr. Hoffman was approximately 5 foot 6 inches tall, with blue eyes, light hair and of light complexion. Mr. Hoffman's monument reads as follows:

Edward Hoffman
Lost His Life In the Viaduct Disaster
November 16, 1895
Aged 23 Yrs & 4 Mos

Mr. Hoffman's wife not only lost her husband, but thereafter their only son Freddie on January 23, 1897, just days before his second birthday. Mr. Hoffman and his son are buried in Section 10, Lot 226.

CONDUCTOR HOFFMAN

Cleveland Press

The 1908 Collinwood School Fire

At Lake View Elementary School on March 4, 1908 school began as usual. At approximately 9:00 AM it was reported that the steam pipes overheated and ignited nearby wood joists. Many of the children and teachers panicked and were later found at the doors. Others tried escaping through the 2nd and 3rd floor windows. Many parents stood on the ground in an attempt to catch the children as they jumped.

A first hand account of the tragedy was relayed by 12 year old Herbert Echelberger /Eichelberger, son of Emmanuel and a student of Miss Lulu M. Rowley, relayed the following story to the *Cleveland Press*:

Author Postcard Collection

"The fire broke out about 10:30. The fire bells in the school rang out, but the boys cried out 'False alarm, false alarm.' Miss Rowley told them to sit still and keep quiet.

At this time the room was filled with smoke and all the children were screaming and yelling; and finally they broke away from the control of the teacher and rushed out in the hall and down the stairways.

When I got into the halls the children were rushing down the stairs, which was jammed full. They were packed in like sardines along the stairway and some were lying down and some were running over those who had fallen.

The flames reached from the basement to the second floor, to where the children were packed on the stairway. Their cries were awful. I don't know whether the doorway had been opened by someone or whether it burned down when I reached there on the first floor.

Herbert Grant and I dove headfirst down the stairway over the mass of children who were lying underneath us. I don't know how I got out. Somebody seemed to grab us and pull us outside.

FIGHTING THE FIRE AT ITS HEIGHT, AFTER THE BUILDING HAD BECOME A FUNERAL PYRE

Author Postcard Collection

I saw little children putting out the fire on their hair with their hands. They were screaming for their parents and teachers, while the flames were creeping all around them. "[43]

When all was said and done, 172 children, two teachers and a rescuer perished in the fire.

Several of the children who were victims in this fire, reside in the cemetery; they are remembered in Table 8.

Florence Ewald was one of the victims. She was the 10 year old daughter of Carl and Bertha Ewald. The parents arrived from Germany in the early 1890's. Florence's headstone has a verse all in German that translates to:

> You bloomed—a flower
> To your Creator's glory.
> Now you are no longer there
> On that day of the Rapture
> Where grownups and children stand
> In the glow of the Heaven's sun
> I want to see you again.

Alvin Sprung was the 7 year old son of Carl and Johanna Sprung. They too were German immigrants in the U.S. for only a short period of time. The Sprungs and Ewalds lived next door to each other according to the 1900 census and both fathers worked for the railroad.

There were 19 children who could not be identified. Collinwood purchased a lot for the burial of these children at Lake View Cemetery. A Memorial Garden has been erected next to the location where the school was located. A plaque can be found in the Memorial Garden with the names of all the children who died as a result of this tragedy.

ALVIN SPRUNG   GRETCHEN TUPPEL   LESTER CENTNER

Cleveland Press

The Shy Family Tragedy

While electronically scanning the burial records at the East Cleveland Service Department, the burial cards for Bertha, age 25; Edward, age 6; and Legree, age 3 stood out from the others. The records indicated that Bertha's throat had been cut with a knife and hatchet and the two young boys had their skulls crushed by a hatchet. The tragic nature of these deaths could not be forgotten.

As it turned out it was Bertha's husband and the father of the two boys who committed these horrible crimes. In *The Evening Telegram* on July 3, 1909 it was reported that Foster Shy, age 31 was being held by the police for having killed his wife and crushed the skulls of his two little boys. It went on to report that Bertha had died within minutes; however, the boys were in St. Alexis Hospital.

The *Cleveland Plain Dealer* reported the tragedy on July 8 and July 9, 1909, indicating that Foster Shy was bound over by the grand jury for the murders of his wife and two children without bond.

The court records document that Mr. Shy was charged first with the murder of his wife on July 10, 1909. Cuyahoga County Common Pleas Court pleadings in case number 1294 found that on July 3, 1909, Foster Shy *"purposely and of deliberate and premeditated malice to kill and murder; and with a certain knife which he, the said Foster Shy, in his right hand then and there had and held, her, the said Bertha Shy, . . . did strike, cut, and wound . . . in and upon the left side of the throat of her, the said Bertha Shy, one mortal wound of the length of about two and one half inches and of the depth of about two inches."* He was not charged for the murders of his two sons until October 1, 1909. In all three cases he was found guilty of murder and sentenced for an undetermined amount of time to the Ohio Penitentiary. The newspaper accounts indicated Mr. Shy had nothing to say regarding the deaths. The court records are limited to the charges and sentence and shed no light on the reason for the murders.

Mr. Shy was found in the 1910 census, listed as an inmate at the Ohio Penitentiary and is where he died on October 10, 1914 of Tuberculosis. The reasons for these murders went to the grave with him as no explanation could be located.

Bertha, Edward and Legree are in unmarked graves located in Section 11, North Plot, Row 15, Grave 131. Not far from their graves, is the grave of Freeman Shy, believed to be the father of Foster, who passed away on July 14, 1909 from a chronic heart condition.

The Cleveland Clinic Tragedy

On May 15, 1929 a fire broke out in the basement of the Cleveland Clinic. The fire was believed to have been caused by an unguarded light bulb hanging near some 70,000 x-ray films stored in manila envelopes on wooden shelves. The burning x-rays caused at least two explosions that released a toxic dense, yellowish-brown cloud of nitrogen and carbon monoxide fumes that filled the building. It was reported that the fumes killed patients on treatment tables and the doctors and nurses collapsed while performing their duties. There were 123 people who perished in this fire, which led to revised safety regulations governing the storage of x-ray films.

The fire is believed to have started due to the light bulb shown in the picture below:

Cleveland Memory Project, Cleveland State University

The scene at the fire is documented below:

Cleveland Memory Project, Cleveland State University

There are two victims of this tragedy in the cemetery, namely, Fabrico Tadiello (Section 13, Lot 117) and Virgil Fleming (Section 2, Lot 124).

Remembering Our Early Settlers

There are over 17,000 residents in East Cleveland Township Cemetery. It would be impossible to tell each of their stories. For the most part, the biographical sketches included are of the early settlers. You will not find stories here of the rich and famous as there were none during the time period in which this is meant to review. These are the stories of the men and women who cleared the land, created the roadways, and built the foundation for the city we now know as Cleveland.

We are a city proud of our cultural diversity, yet it is believed that we do not always focus our attention on the New England born early settlers and what they had to endure and accomplish to build a city that would experience mass immigration from Europe in the mid to late 1800's; for the creation of what we remember as Millionaire's Row and for the city we enjoy today. These earlier settlers were predominantly from the original thirteen colonies and were descendents of the families that were the original settlers of the United States.

C.O. Barlett remembered our early settlers at the 1931 Early Settlers Association meeting as follows:

> *Few of us realize the great work done by our early settlers of a hundred and more years ago, and the influence of their labor in many ways. They were a wonderful people: honorable, capable, well- and self-educated, and very industrious; in fact, such a people could and did set a splendid example for their children to follow.*
>
> *The first ambition of these sturdy pioneers was to get a home, which is almost universally regarded as one of the most important*

aims in life and which is recognized everywhere as the basis for a happy and prosperous community. The country, to be sure, was an unbroken forest, which meant hard work and much self-denial; but it offered many advantages as well. The fine timber gave the best material for good, comfortable cabins and barns.

Many of the trees were nut trees, which furnished excellent food for hogs, and which, in turn, provided food for the settlers. Also, wild game was plentiful, especially deer and wild turkeys. The maples gave sap for sugar; the rich land, when cleared, produced the best of wheat, corn and potatoes.

All these factors encourage home-owning, and that habit was cultivated in their children and grandchildren, so that today Cleveland has a higher per cent of home-owners than any other large city in the United States.

These New England pioneers were well-educated and self-educated in the common branches of education; and their second consideration was to provide schools for their children. They cooperated in building their own log schoolhouses, and their daughters were educated and capable of teaching the three R's in a manner which made things stick. Their wages were necessarily very small, for money was scarce, and frequently taught for board and less than a dollar a week.[44]

So sit back and take a brief look at some of our early settlers and their accomplishments.

Daniel M. Alvord– Mr. Alvord was born in Lake County on April 15, 1847 the son of D.J. and Mary Ann (nee Turner) Alvord. Daniel left the Lake county family farm at the age of nineteen to work for the Lake Shore & Michigan Southern Railroad Company. His employment with the railroad ceased when he enlisted in Company C, 150th Regiment and was stationed at Washington, District of Columbia in Fort Bunker Hill until his discharge in September 1864.

Mr. Alvord married Sarah M. (nee Wilcox) on November 16, 1873. He moved the family briefly to Iowa but returned to Cleveland and the

Lake Shore & Michigan Southern Railroad Company after contracting malaria. Their children were George, David and Florence.

He was a member of the Thatcher Lodge, No. 439, A.F. & A.M. of Nottingham; also of Division 20 of the O.R.C. and was its first Secretary and Treasurer. Mr. and Mrs. Alvord, along with their son David reside in Section 10, Lot 41.

Luther Battles, Jr. – Mr. Battles was born April 29, 1826 in Herkimer County, New York, the son of Luther (Sr.) and Arathusa (nee Porter) Battles. Mr. Battles was considered a "worthy representative of one of the oldest families of Cuyahoga County." He married Catherine Mapes on December 1, 1847 and they had five children. Mrs. Battles was born on January 14, 1827, the daughter of Rufus and Abigail (nee Allen) Mapes. Mrs. Mapes was a direct descendent of Ethan Allen.

On September 8, 1888 at a family reunion Luther Battles, Jr. recalled the family's journey to the Western Reserve:

> *It is now fifty-three years since our father and mother with their eight children started from Herkimer town and county, New York, for their comparatively wilderness home in Ohio, Cuyahoga county, situated on the east bank of the Chagrin river, in the town of Mayfield, and now known as a part of the East Hill. They came from Utica to Buffalo by canal, and from Buffalo here in a wagon drawn by a pair of gray horses, -- to our long talked of home. With little or no money, strangers among strangers, with no revenue save the products of their own industry, they depended upon their own efforts for everything. They did not expect manna to fall in the wilderness for them, nor loaves to come to their baskets, or fishes to their nets, without an effort of their own; so they taught us that we would not reap if we did not sow. Now they commenced the long and weary struggle for life anew; hardships were encountered on every hand, but they had an indomitable will that never deviated from the main object, which was to conquer the wilds of nature and provide for the wants of their household; and whatever measure of success crowned their lives was the direct result of their own*

vigorous efforts; out of the storms of effort came forth sunshine; out of the bitter came forth sweet.

Mr. and Mrs. Battles reside in Section 10, Lot 91, along with several children and grandchildren.

Richard H. Blinn (original subscriber in the Publick Burying Ground) came to the Cleveland area in 1799; information regarding his life prior to his arrival in Cleveland could not be located. In 1802 Mr. Blinn married Sarah Doan, the daughter of Nathaniel and Sarah Adams Doan. He served in the War of 1812, as a Private in 1 Regiment (Beard's), Ohio Militia. They had one son who was named Nathaniel Doan Blinn, after Mrs. Blinn's father. Sarah Doan Blinn passed away at an early age, and Mr. Blinn married a second time to Electa Hamilton, the daughter of Samuel and Susannah Hamilton. The couple had at least six (6) children.

In approximately 1818 Mr. Blinn began to build a new home just north of the Edwards Tavern on what was then Woodhill Road. Ahimaaz Sherwin, Jr. assisted Mr. Blinn with the carpentry work.

The family moved to Perrysburg, Ohio and only limited information could be located. It is known that Nathaniel Doan Blinn was still living in Perrysburg according to the 1860 census with his wife, Maria and 19-year-old daughter Mary. His occupation was listed as a farmer.

Abbey Burton(second wife of Dr. Elijah Burton) - Abbey was born in Vermont the daughter of Elijah Hollister who was one of the pioneers of Manchester, was an early sheriff of Bennington County, and who also served in the War of 1812. Mrs. Burton spoke to the Early Settlers Association in 1882 and told of her arrival in Cleveland:

I came to the Reserve in 1824 in a vessel; landed in Cleveland the third day of May, about five in the evening; Captain Williamson commanded the vessel was obliged to cast anchor three miles out; no wharves or docks; came ashore in a small boat. The captain hesitated about trying to come on shore until morning, but finally he says: "If you dare venture, I will take two sailors and your trunk." We had no such mammoth trunks as there are in this age. There were a hundred and sixty passengers, and most of them sea-sick. I said I would as soon be at the bottom of Lake Erie as to be here; we made the attempt, and got on shore all right. The captain took me up to Doctor McIntosh, who then kept public house. There we found Doctor Burton and Rodney Strong, the doctor on horseback, and Mr. Strong in a buggy, who very kindly gave me a ride to Euclid, now Collamer. The road was very full of stumps, the trees were cut, but the stumps were still standing. After going about two miles there came up a heavy thunder-shower; we were in total darkness, only when it lightened. The doctor was directly behind us, urging us on, but we arrived safe at Mr. Strong's door at eight in the evening; he was then keeping public house in the Lyndley House, now torn down; this was Saturday evening. Sunday, at noon, Mr. Adams came there, and after an introduction, he invited me to go to church with him –a nice old gentleman, Mr. Darius Adams' father—he said he would give me the best seat in the church. I went. He seated me with General Dille and wife on a buggy seat that they had brought in for their own convenience. The minister was the Rev. Mr. Bradstreet; he boarded in our family, Doctor Burton's.

The next week I attended a dancing party at the house of Mr. David Bonnell, quite a small log house. It stood where Mr. Harbeck's house now stands. The musician was Mr. James Hendershot—splendid music. I enjoyed it much; all plain, happy people—no strife for dress or fashion. The same week the school directors came for me to teach the school in Frogville, now Collinwood; went down in an ox team; the roads were just logs thrown together, very rough. I taught three months; boarded in Mr. Hale's family, now all dead. Among the scholars was a large, hardy young chap. I was often amused, standing at the window to see him crack chestnut burs with his heel. He is now an honorable member of your Association.

Very few of the old settlers are left. I could mention many interesting circumstances of the early settlers. When the Doctor arrived at Euclid he had but two shillings left. He and another young man *flipped a copper to see which should have the district school; it fell to the Doctor's lot to teach the school, and by that means he got into practice and was very successful.*

I will take no more time. Mrs. A.P. Burton; Collamer, Aug. 20, 1882

Note: It may not be improper to state that the writer of the foregoing is the widow of Dr. Elijah Burton, deceased, who for many years was a resident physician of Euclid township. He came to Euclid in 1820, taught the school for awhile, and studied medicine with Dr. Farnsworth, a physician of that vicinity. Dr. Burton soon acquired an enviable reputation as a medical practitioner, and especially in diseases peculiar to a new country. He was a noble-hearted man, kind and liberal, and highly respected by all who knew him. He died in 1854.[45]

Mrs. Abbey Burton passed away in 1889.

Dr. Elijah Burton - Dr. Burton was born in approximately 1793 and came to East Cleveland in approximately 1820 from Manchester, Bennington County, Vermont with his wife Mary. Dr. Burton served as a Sergeant in the regular Army during the War of 1812, while a resident of Manchester.[46] Mary Burton passed away in 1827 in Cleveland and he subsequently married Abbey Hollister Burton.[47]

Dr. Burton made his home on Euclid Avenue, where he resided until his death in 1854. He was a highly respected doctor in the area for many years, with his son and thereafter his grandson all practicing medicine in Cleveland for a period of approximately 99 years.

Dr. Elijah Burton, his son and his grandson were physicians who practiced through 99 successive years in the neighborhood of Collamer. During a third of that time, father and son lived side by side west of Nobel road on the south side of Euclid Avenue, then a road. For years they occupied the same office on the family lot. The grandson lived not far east and the combined practice of the trio extended from 1820 to 1919.

Dr. Elijah Burton was born in Manchester, Bennington County, Vermont, in 1793. Seeking a location in the west at the age of 27, he rode into East Cleveland, his saddlebags filled with medicine. Already he was a practitioner, married and the father of a child. Arriving in Euclid Township, later Collamer, with but a quarter in cash he flipped a coin with another newcomer to decide who should teach in a proposed school. The doctor won, took the position and built the log school. During the one year of his teaching he fought the school bully and threw him into the burning logs of the fireplace.

Dr. Burton taught five days weekly, visiting patients out of school hours, and after a night with a patient, it was not unusual for him to drop asleep while hearing lessons. He had attended lectures in Castleton, Vt, and had practiced there and after further studied here, he devoted all his time to his profession. In 1821 he sent for his wife, Mary Hollister Burton, and their four-year-old daughter, Lucy A. Burton. Mrs. Burton, gentle and delicate, sang in the village choir, as did her daughter. The mother lived only six years after coming west and was buried in the old church cemetery once at the corner of E. 105th Street and Euclid Avenue. Lucy Burton married George Croghan Dodge, father of Samuel Douglas Dodge, now residing in Mentor.

Dr. Burton then married Abigail Hollister, sister of his first wife, who came to East Cleveland in 1824 as a girl of 19 and was called "Abby" by her friends. An only child of this marriage, Mary Burton, remained unmarried. The doctor became Colonel of the local militia and his "rides" to attend the sick now extended in a circuit of over 10 miles. In the summer of 1834, cholera prevailed in the region and Squire Job Doan was taken sick. Representative from the county, the previous June, he had been appointed postmaster of the new office at Doan's Corners. Dr. Burton attended him but Job Doan died on the morning of Sept. 20, 1834. The physician himself was seized with the disease and was violently sick for three days. He treated himself and as he recovered his entire company marched to his home in military formation.

On a ride in the vicinity of Doan's Corners, after a birth it was discovered that there was no whisky for jollification and no receptacle to bring it in. The doctor took a pigskin bag from the cabin wall, sent it to the nearest source of supply and regaled assembled friends.

A leading Democrat, the young physician exercised a large influence on campaigns and was consulted on the probable outcome of elections. In 1846 his son, Dr. E. D. Burton, became his associate in medical practice.

The two had an office in the common yard in which their homes stood. The son was 21 when he joined his father in the partnership which continued eight years until the death of the elder Burton in 1854. The latter was a man of native force and marked characteristics, and traditions long remained in the neighborhood of his energy and wit.

Mrs. Abby Burton lived many years in Collamer, dying July 9, 1889 at the age of 85. She had seen Euclid Avenue cleared of stumps, lived long in the time of plank roads and tollgates, witnessed the building of the "Dummy" line as a quick means of reaching Cleveland, and the Nickel Plate Railway was running trains through the hamlet during the last decade of her life.[48]

The early doctors of the Western Reserve usually had not attended medical school to earn their credentials to treat our early settlers. The details of a doctor's training were provided by Dr. Frederick C. Waite in 1931:

. . . . . . It was entirely by the apprenticeship or preceptorial system.

What were the essentials of this method? The boy of 16 to 18 enrolled as an apprentice or student under a practicing physician. For a period of at least three years this relation continued. In the earliest days it continued for seven years. At the first, the boy was occupied with menial duties, such as looking after the doctor's horses, hoeing his garden, and things of that kind. He spent part of each day studying the few books which the doctor owned, and at night would recite to the doctor, who was called his preceptor. His study of medicine started with anatomy. During a few weeks of one winter, in some retired barn loft, the doctor and student would dissect a human body, surreptitiously secured from some potter's field or distant churchyard.

With mortar and pestle the student would grind the crude drugs so essential to the treatment in those days, and then would help the doctor make those mixtures and parcel out the doses, which were bulky and efficacious, although not very palatable. While the student was doing these things he was constantly getting oral instructions as to the properties and actions of these drugs. (I recall, and I don't go back to 1800, but I well recall, as a boy, taking a half a teacup-ful of a pasty mixture of rhubarb, jalap and senna, to which, as an unpalatable mixture, I have never found a rival.)

On the doctor's daily rounds the student would drive the doctor's hors and chaise. As time went on, he would accompany the doctor to the sick room first as a mere observer, then as an assistant in the simpler, and, finally, in the more difficult cases. On rare occasions he would assist at an amputation of a leg or arm, and last of all, would be permitted to assist at obstetric cases.

His next promotion was to visit some of the doctor's convalescing patients, to deliver new supplies of medicine, and report on progress, and finally, in times of many demands, he would be sent to care for the apparently less serious cases, or to those few families where the predilection for the "old doctor" and lack of confidence in the "young doctor" was not too strong.

The time finally would come when his preceptor felt his student could go alone. He would then give him a certificate of efficiency and a recommending letter addressed "To whom it may concern," and the young man, as soon as he could grow a beard to dissimulate his youthfulness, was ready to begin independent practice.[49]

Dr. Burton and both his wives are buried next to each other in Section 3, Lot 43.

Philip Cody– Mr. Cody was born on July 1, 1770 in Massachusetts. His wife was Lydia (nee Martin) Cody. S. J. Kelly chronicles the story of the Cody family in *"Buffalo Bill's Grandfather was Cleveland Pioneer"*.

> *Phillip Cody, grandfather of Buffalo Bill, was an early settler of the Western Reserve with his wife. He came to Cleveland from Toronto, Canada, in 1812 and became owner of a large farm in East Cleveland Township, near what is now E. 86th Street. He died in 1850 and was buried in the churchyard of the old Congregational Church at the corner of Euclid and E. 105th.*
>
> *In walking through those toppling tombstones I have seen the ones marked "Phillip Cody and Lydia Martin Cody, his wife." The graveyard was on the ground now occupied by the Alhambra Theater. When the site of the church and yard was taken over by the present buildings, Mr. Harry B. Cody of 2603 Norfolk Road, a great-grandson, removed his ancestors to East Cleveland Cemetery where they now rest.*

Cleveland Press Collection, Cleveland State University

Despite the story that has been started that the famed scout, Buffalo Bill, was of foreign birth, his father, Isaac Cody, first saw the light of day in Cuyahoga County, within what are now the limits of the city. The old Cody farm fronted on Euclid Avenue where the Sears-Roebuck store is located. There were four sons of the first Phillip Cody, Isaac, Elijah, Joseph and Phillip. Isaac was born in 1813. With his brothers Elijah and Philip, he left the city for the west about 1838.

Isaac Cody married Mary Ann Leacock and settled on a small farm in Scott County, Iowa. Here the future plainsman, Indian fighter and showman, William Frederick Cody, "Buffalo Bill," was born in a roomy cabin Feb. 26, 1846. His father started with some belated forty-niners for California but turned back. In 1854, the family moved westward, crossed the Missouri near the frontier Fort Leavenworth, Kan. A few miles farther on, Isaac Cody entered the wooded Salt Creek Valley, felled trees and built a cabin. They were on the Great Salt Lake Trail. Before the door passed prairie schooners, stage coaches, tardy gold seekers, guides, trappers, scouts and soldiers. A few miles farther west began the plains stretching to the Rockies, roamed by herds of buffalo. The remnants of eastern tribes of Indians, and all he warlike tribes west of the Mississippi, hunted the great prairies north and south. It was their big reservation by treaty and agreement with the government.

Did seven-year old Buffalo Bill fall in with the situation? He kicked in on everything. His father gave him a pony and he was thrown heels over head, but learned to ride. He played with the Kickapoo Indian boys from their reservation made bows and arrows and learned to throw the lariat. He rode around with bustling border men engaged in assembling those long covered wagon trains going west, and became all wrapped up in the mules, horses, cattle and teamsters. His uncle Elijah Cody, had some time before established a store at Weston on the Missouri shore. Isaac Cody, an abolitionist, was drawn into making a speech in 1855, during Kansas' pro-slavery times and was stabbed in the back by an employee of his brother's store. Subject to persecution, he went to Grasshopper Falls, a free state settlement. Still suffering from his *wound he visited Ohio. Then he returned to Kansas and died in 1857.*

It devolved upon young Bill Cody, then barely 11 years old, to help support the family. He started across the plains with an outfit that was herding a drove of beef cattle to Utah and engaged in his first Indian fight.

To tell how Bill Cody became a trapper, guide, scout and chief of scouts; of his lone racing night rides over the prairie and through hostile tribes, bearing messages from fort to fort for Gen. Phil Sheridan; of his fights and skirmishes with the Indians, and of his single-handed combats with big chiefs, would fill a score of volumes like "Deadwood Dick." To tell how he won his title of Buffalo Bill, how he became the most famous scout of the west and guided James Gordon Bennett and the Grand Duke Alexis on hunting trips, would take chapter after chapter.

It should be told, however, how young Bill Cody at 15 was sent back to Cleveland to get him away from the plains and to attend school. He did not stay very long, soon said goodby and left for the west.

Years ago I talked to Lindus Cody, son of Dr. Phillip Cody and cousin of the famous scout, at this home where Vine Road leaves Lake Shore Boulevard East (Route 283). If you ever have talked to Lindus Cody you would say that in looks, manner and action he was exactly like Buffalo Bill.

Philip and Lydia Cody were transferred from the Publick Burying Ground to Section 10, Lot 157 in East Cleveland Township Cemetery. While searching for the marker shown above the markers for their daughter Elizabeth, who passed away on October 30, 1847, and grand-daughter Emma, who passed away on May 6, 1841, were located in the same Section and Lot about 2 feet under ground. Elizabeth had married William Custead.

Author Photograph Collection

Author Photograph Collection

Henry H. Coit– Mr. Coit was born June 17, 1791 in Norwich, Connecticut, the son of Daniel Lathrop Coit. Daniel L. Coit was a member of the Western Reserve Land Company and he owned all of Liverpool, Medina County; 1,000 acres in Euclid (which became East

Cleveland) and approximately 1,000 acres in Lorain County. Henry came to the Western Reserve in 1814, leaving a position in a counting room in New York. He married Mary (nee Breed) in 1814. They continued to live in Liverpool until approximately 1830 at which time they moved to East Cleveland. In 1837 a village in Medina County that was called Marysville was named after Henry's wife. The village declined and was eventually absorbed into the adjacent farms.

Mr. Coit's property in what was East Cleveland was 1,000 acres of lake front property. He was a very skilled horticulturist and floriculturist, with the grounds surrounding his mansion being the envy of everyone in the county.

Mr. Coit also served this area as a member of the Ohio Militia. On November 13, 1818 he was promoted to Major of the Third Regiment of the Third Brigade, Fourth Division; thereafter on March 2, 1822 he was promoted to Lieutenant Colonel of the Fifth Regiment, in the Third Brigade, Fourth Division of the Ohio Militia.

Mr. Coit, his wife Mary and son Charles Breed Coit rest in Section 6, Lot 17.

Rev. Thomas Corlett – At the 1890 meeting of the Early Settlers Association of Cuyahoga County, Rev. A.B. Putnam, remembered his friend Thomas Corlett who passed away on August 30, 1889:

> *And now what he did for others it falls to others to do for him. The workers fail and drop by the way, but the organized work still goes on. When the last annual meeting was held, his interest in the affairs of this Association was so great that he postponed a trip for his health in order to attend to his duties as Chaplain, and then within less than forty days, by the providence of God, he was taken to his eternal home.*
>
> *As his Rector, it was my good fortune to know him well during his latter days on earth, to minister to him in spiritual things, to enjoy his confidence and conversation, and when the end came to be at his bedside and commend his departing soul to the everlasting mercy of God. The days of his pilgrimage were more than three score years and ten, and the whole period was passed in the loyal*

service of his heavenly King, whom he loved with all his heart and followed with rare devotion.

Mr. Corlett was a native of the picturesque and historically interesting Isle-of-Man, where he was born September 28, 1817. When only ten years of age his parents came to Cleveland, attracted by the prospects and future growth of population and commercial interests, purchased a home and settled down in Newburgh.

Many of the inconveniences and hardships incident to the life of Early Settlers were familiar to them, and as a proof of the frugality and thriftiness, as well as the independence of young Corlett, it is only necessary to state that when he left home to seek an education, with the exception of a good trade he possessed only fifteen dollars, with which to support himself, but when he graduated he had saved eleven hundred dollars from his earnings, over and above his expenses. During the years that followed he had an extended and successful experience as a teacher, and many of those who received from him the first earnest desire to excel in knowledge and virtue are ready to rise up and call him blessed. Being persuaded that it was his duty to enter the Holy Ministry, he gave up his school work, was ordained to the Diaconate and Priesthood by Bishop McIlvaine, and served as a Clergyman of the Protestant Episcopal Church, for many years in Ohio, and for a short time at Barraboo, Wisconsin. But Ohio was his home by choice as well as in fact, and nearly all his life was passed in the vicinity of Cleveland, among the friends and companions of his boyhood days.

He was Rector of St. Paul's Church, Collamer several times, Assistant Minister of Trinity Church Cleveland, when the venerable Dr. Bolles was Rector, and in charge of St. Peter's Church. Dwelling among the people by whom he was best known both in the active exercise of the ministry and in private life, when failing health made retirement necessary, his influence was of the most healthful kind. In him there was an unfailing supply of the "milk of human kindness," sweetened by the grace which comes through the Gospel of Peace. The sterling qualities which he inherited from his ancestors did not fail him during his long life. Fidelity to trust, *loyal allegiance to friends, singular purity of life without austerity, remarkable sweetness and calmness of disposition, all were marks of a character of a native strength which had been purified and ennobled by discipline and the Grace of God. He was, without any qualification, a "good man, full of the Holy Ghost and of faith," and when the end came he was fully prepared to enter into the joy of his Lord. Such characters are "the salt of the earth." They exemplify the value of love and gentleness and a holy life. They are the most powerful forces in society, reaching out to the weary and heavy burdened, leaving to the world the legacy and benediction which can only result from a life pure and without reproach. Slow to anger and of marked compassion was our friend, loth to believe ill concerning anyone, full of that highest of all God's gifts, an ever-abounding charity, spread out like a mantle to cover faults and shortcomings and sins. He was a notable example of high-minded Christian manhood. We cherish his memory. We love to speak of his excellencies of character.*

The closing words of his last annual report, which are familiar to all those who use the Liturgy, which he loved with unshaken devotion, may well be our last words to-day:

May we who still survive be so guided and helped in our work of life by the Divine blessing, that when we are called hence we may, with all those who are departed in the true faith of God's holy name, have our perfect consummation and bliss, both in body and soul, in His eternal and everlasting glory, through Jesus Christ our Lord.[50]

Rev. Corlett resides in Section 5, Lot 27 with other members of his family.

Andrew Cozad was born in 1801 in Prosperity, Washington County, Pennsylvania. He moved to Cleveland with his parents, Samuel, Jr. and Jane (nee McIlrath) Cozad, in approximately 1806. Andrew and his brother Elias inherited a number of 100-acre lots that spanned the area from Doan's Corner to Lake View Cemetery. Andrew married Sally

Simmons of Fredonia, New York. They had nine children: Jane Celesta, Mary Ann, Nathaniel Clark, Justus L., Charlotte, Andrew Dudley, Henry Irving, Sarah L (Duty) and Marcus Eugene. A portion of the 100-acre lot number 396 originally belonged to Andrew Cozad prior to being broken and sold as several individual parcels of land.

In 1835 Andrew Cozad was appointed one of the administrators of the trust that included 90 acres of land bequest by John Shaw for The Shaw Academy (now known as Shaw High School). The 1860 and 1870 census, Andrew is listed as a farmer by trade. The value of his property increased in value from $25,000 to $50,000 over that 10-year period of time. Mr. Cozad passed away on May 20, 1873 and is buried in Lake View Cemetery, Section 6, Lot 66.

Hiram Day – Mr. Day was born on September 10, 1810 in Washington County, Pennsylvania and arrived in Cleveland on his third birthday, September 10, 1813, the day of the Battle of Put-in-Bay i.e. Battle of Lake Erie, with his parents Benjamin and Nancy (nee Andrews) Day. The cannons from the Battle underway could be heard out over the lake; the settlers had everything ready to "*beat a hasty retreat*" just in case the Americans lost the day.

Benjamin Day purchased 333 acres of heavily wooded land. The task of clearing the land was grueling work. Their nearest neighbors were Indians with bear, wolves and deer roaming freely.

Hiram married first on November 10, 1837 to Catherine Bishop who was born in East Cleveland. She passed away on May 10, 1845. Mr. Day married a second time to Deborah Albee also of East Cleveland. Two children were born of each marriage.

Mr. Day passed away May 23, 1896. Mr. Day, both wives and a number of his children reside in Section 12, Lots 29 and 30. His son Joseph A. Day can be found in the family lot as well. His headstone proudly reports on his 34 years in railway mail service.

Samuel Dibble (original subscriber in the Publick Burying Ground) was 18 years of age when he arrived in Cleveland with his parents, Elisha and Phebe Stone Dibble in 1812. The War of 1812 broke out shortly after their arrival in Cleveland. Samuel and Elisha joined the war effort. Elisha became extremely ill while serving. He returned home and died shortly thereafter. When the War ended Samuel returned to take care of his mother and eight other siblings. He married twice while in Cleveland. The first marriage is reported to have been to Miss Jewett and the second to Susana Tibbets.

Mr. Dibble was still living in Cleveland according to the 1830 census; however, by the 1840 census he and his family had moved to Elkhart County, Indiana.

Dille Family -- Two brothers, David, Jr. and Asa left Washington County, Pennsylvania and traveled to Cleveland.

David, Jr. was born in 1753, was a veteran of the Revolutionary War, having served two terms as a Lieutenant in the Virginia Militia under Colonel Crawford against the Indians.[51] Mr. Dille was the second settler in Euclid when he arrived in November, 1798. He passed away in 1853 and is buried in Euclid Cemetery.

Mr. Dille had two wives and at least 16 children. The records indicate a potential that there were 22 children, 18 of which reached maturity.[52] Three of David and Nancy Vier Dille's sons are buried in East Cleveland Township Cemetery, namely Nehemiah, Luther and Asa.

Nehemiah was born in 1781, the eldest child of David and Nancy Viers Dille. Very little information could be located on Nehemiah. What was located indicates that after his arrival in Cleveland, he lived his life in Euclid and held several different positions in the governance of Euclid that included Constable, Trustee of the Euclid Township, and fence viewer. For the position of Constable it was recorded he was paid $1.50 in 1815. In 1822 Mr. Dille collected $3.00 in fines for breaches of peace. He and his family are buried in Section 1, Lot 4.

Luther was born in 1785. In early Euclid there were many large pits of rattlesnakes. The rattlesnakes were hazardous to the early settlers and young boys were just as curious then as they are today.

> *Boy-like they experimented with the reptile. One boy bet that he could touch the tail of a snake and get away without being bitten. He tried it to his sorrow, but his life was saved by quick and heroic treatment. The boys would often hold the reptiles down with a forked stock, then slip a noose of tough bark over their heads and*

take them home as live captives to show and shock the family. They shot many with the bow and arrow. It is due to this active and energetic campaign against them that the pioneers coming into this infested region suffered so few losses by snake bite, but the presence of the reptiles was a drawback and their destruction a part of pioneer history.[53]

Luther was credited with killing forty-three rattlesnakes and became so sick from the fumes of the rattlesnakes that he had to stop before the snake pit was cleared.

Luther served on the first jury in Cuyahoga County Common Pleas Court, which was held in June, 1810. The trial involved recovery of money paid for eight barrels of whitefish which was found to be damaged.[54] He also served in the War of 1812 in Captain Harvey Murray's Company as a Private from August 21 to November 30, 1812.[55]

Luther and his second wife Clarissa were one of the first members of the Disciple Church of Collamer that was organized in 1829. He married Clarissa on September 7, 1828, shortly after the death of his first wife Esther. He had served as bishop of the church for over 30 years at the time of his passing in 1863.[56]

In the 1860 census he was living in Euclid, with his son, Eri M and his family. Luther passed away on April 19, 1863; he is buried in Section 1, Lot 12 along with his wives; his son Eri, and Eri's wife Emeline.

Asa was born in Washington County, Pennsylvania in 1788. He married Mary Johnson. In the 1850 census Asa is listed as living in Euclid with an occupation of farmer. Asa, his wife and children are buried in Section 6, Lots 6 and 35.

David, Jr's brother, Asa, arrived in the Cleveland area in March of 1804. He was the second actual settler in East Cleveland.[57] Asa was the first treasurer appointed by the Cuyahoga County Commissioners. Asa also had a large family, his son Jacob was a cooper by trade. A cooper today would refer to a barrel-maker. The cooper made containers for flour, gun-powder and other commodities. This was a trade that was usually passed down from one generation to the next.

In the case of Jacob, he transferred this trade to his son Julius. Julius was born in approximately 1826. The 1860 census documents Julius and his father working as coopers. Jacob, his wife Eleanor, son Julius, Julius' wives and other family members reside in Section 8, Lot 23.

Anna Olivia (nee Baldwin) Doane – Mrs. Doane was the daughter of Seth Cogswell Baldwin, the Revolutionary War veteran mentioned earlier. She married John Doane, the son of Timothy Doane in January, 1820. The wedding was a double wedding with her brother Edward marrying Mercy Doan, the daughter of Nathaniel Doan.

Her obituary as it appeared in the *Cleveland Herald* on February 27, 1821 read as follows:

> *Died Euclid the 25 inst., Mrs. Ann Olivia Doan, wife of Mr. John Doan and daughter of S.C. Baldwin, Esq., of Cleaveland, in the 19th year of her age.*
>
> *This stroke of Divine Providence leaves a beloved husband to mourn the loss of the friend of his heart – to the tender father and relatives, an afflicting dispensation.*
>
> > *How lv'd or valued, now avails thee not,*
> > *To whom related, or by whom begot,*
> > *A heap of dust alone remains of thee,*
> > *Tis all thou art, and all that we shall be.*

Mrs. Doane was buried in Section 6, Lot 11 with her husband and his parents.

Timothy Doane, Sr Family – Given the fact that nearly everyone knew the Doane/Doan family in the Western Reserve, it seems appropriate to let John Doane (son of Timothy Sr.) and the people that knew them tell his family story. The history of the Doane family was read to the Early Settlers Association in 1881 as follows:

> *John Doane, of Collamer, the oldest living pioneer of Cuyahoga county, came to Cleveland in April, 1801. He was born June 28, 1798, and consequently is now almost eighty-three years of age,*

although he looks to be much younger. The distinction of being the oldest male inhabitant of the county invests Mr. Doane with public interest, and the facts regarding both his ancestors and his life while here will be read with pleasure. Mr. Doane is descended from one of the oldest families in the country, and his family for generations has supplied substantial and worthy members of the community. While heredity does not possess the significance in this country that it does abroad, it is always a matter to be gratified at that our ancestors have been useful men and good citizens. The original John Doane, the founder of the Doane family in this country, crossed the Atlantic in one of the first three ships that sailed to Plymouth, landing at that famous spot in the year 1636. A brother came after and settled in Canada, and founded a family that now has numerous branches in the Dominion. Another brother settled in Virginia, and also founded an extensive connection.

John Doane, the ancestor, took a prominent and useful part in the affairs of Plymouth colony, and in 1633 was chosen assistant to Governor Winslow. Subsequently in 1639 he was chosen one of the Commissioners to revise the laws. In 1642 he was again made assistant to the Governor, and in 1647 and for several years succeeding he was elected Deputy to the Colony Court. In addition to the civil offices which he held he was made a deacon in the church at Plymouth and at Eastham. He died in 1685 at the advanced age of ninety-five years. His wife's name was Abigail, and by her he had five children--Lydia, Abigail, John, Ephraim and Daniel. All of these were the progenitors of large families, whose descendants are numerous in that section.

Daniel Doane had four children by his first wife, among whom was Joseph Doane, who was born June 27th, 1669, three years after the fire and plague of London. Joseph had twelve children by two wives. He was a deacon of the church at Eastham for forty years, and was a pious and God-fearing man. His first child was named Mary, after her mother, and the second Joseph, after the father.

Joseph Jr., was born November 15th, 1693 and married Deborah Haddock, September 30th, 1725. He moved to Middle Haddam, near Middletown, on the Connecticut river, and there engaged in ship building. His children were Joseph, Nathaniel, Seth, Eunice and Phineas. Seth was born June 9th, 1733, and married Mercy Parker, February 23d, 1758. Both died in 1802. They had nine children, Seth, Timothy, Elizabeth, Nathaniel, Job (died early), Mercy, Job, John M. and Deborah. The two Seth Doanes, father and son, were taken prisoners by the British from a merchant vessel in 1776, during the Revolutionary war, the father, at the time, being mate of the vessel on which he was captured. They were released in 1777, and soon after the younger Seth died from sickness contracted while a prisoner and due to his captivity.

Nearly all of these children came west and settled in and around Cleveland. Nathaniel was the first Doane to reach this vicinity. He came here in 1796 with a surveying party and in 1798 moved with his family. The route of emigration was down the Connecticut river, along the coast by vessel to New York, up the Hudson river, across by land to Lake Ontario, and thence by boat to the mouth of the Cuyahoga river. The family lived in the then little village of Cleveland, until the next fall, when they removed to what is now East Cleveland, settling at the 'Corners,' just this side of Wade Park. The children of Nathaniel Doane were Sarah, Job (died young), Delia, Nathaniel and Mercy. W. H. Doane, of Cleveland, is a son of Job Doane.

Timothy Doane moved from Connecticut to Herkimer county, New York, about the year 1794. In 1801 he followed his brother Nathaniel to Cleveland, arriving here in April. On the way he stopped at Fairport, where his journey from Buffalo stopped. From Fairport he and his family performed the journey on horseback to Cleveland. Timothy's family consisted of himself and wife, and six children-Nancy, Seth, Timothy, Mary, Deborah and John. Of these only one besides John is living--Deborah the mother of T. D. Crocker, who was born January 14, 1796. Nancy Doane married Samuel Dodge, the father of General H.H. and George C. Dodge.

Seth married Lucy Clark, and was the father of David Clark Doane, Margaret A., wife of A.S. Gardner and Seth Cary Doane. Children of each of them reside in Cleveland. Timothy had eleven children, whose descendants reside mostly in East Cleveland.

John, the subject of the present sketch, was born in 1798 and having been brought to Cleveland in 1801, has been a resident here for 78 years. There were only a few log huts here at the time, and the country was very wild. It is a somewhat noteworthy circumstance that he has lived within one hundred yards of the same spot where he now resides since 1801.

In January, 1820, John married Olivia Baldwin, who lived but a short time. In September, 1832, he married Sophia Taylor, and by her had six children--Mary S., Abigail Cordelia, Edward B., Anna O., Harriet S., and John Willis, all of whom are living and reside in or near Cleveland.

He has been a witness of all the principal events of local interest from the building of the first frame house in the county to the present time. He saw the Indian Omic hung in 1812, and has a distinct recollection of the event, as it occurred on the Square, nearly in front of where J. M. Richards & Co.'s establishment is now. A storm came on during the hanging of Omic, and he was cut down and the body put into a box, which, it was afterward ascertained, the doctors got hold of at night.

Mr. Doane has been a Republican in politics ever since the organization of the party. He has never taken an active interest in politics, to which is probably due much of his good health and peace of mind. He is to-day one of the most active old men in the county. He gets around in a lively manner, and is; generally on the go. He has never used tobacco in any form, nor has he ever indulged in ardent spirits. He attributes his longevity and health to daily exercise and regular habits.

Mr. Doane's present home is just east of the Euclid Avenue House, while the old Doane farm, where he lived so many years, is directly opposite. The majority of Doanes in this section spell their names without the final letter of the original name; a custom that

*was introduced some fifty or more years since, and has been kept up
by all the families here except by the descendants of John Doane.*[58]

Mr. Doane spoke to the Early Settlers Association of Cuyahoga
County in 1886 regarding his early memories of life in Cleveland:

> *Cleveland, as I first remember it, this in answer to a question,
> contained only four houses. One was Lorenzo Carter's log dwelling
> on a small knoll a short distance below what is, now Water street,
> on St. Clair. It was a common, old-fashioned log house. He subse-
> quently built a house near the corner of Water and Superior streets.
> When it was well under way the men who were employed upon it
> went down to the old house for breakfast, I think, and while they
> were gone the structure in some way caught fire and burned to the
> ground. Then he went into the woods and hewed timber and put
> up another house, the outside of which was afterwards boarded
> over. It was in this that Omic, the Indian, was chained prior to
> his execution on the Public Square. He was a great curiosity, and I
> remember going in to see him with the rest. I was then about four-
> teen years of age, and as curious as are most youngsters of that age.
> As to the four houses I spoke of, in my first recollection of Cleve-
> land, Carter's old log was one, Squire Spafford's, on the south side
> of Superior street, was the second, and I cannot name the others. It
> was then all woods on Superior street at the square, and that was
> also covered with forest.*
>
> *My father built the second house erected in Euclid township, a
> man named Burke having put up the first. When we came down
> here we were located within forty or fifty rods of a camp of Indians.
> They never molested us, and I can remember seeing four or five of
> them at once around the fire at my father's. They made no objec-
> tions to our occupancy of the land, although they did claim the
> ownership of that on the West Side of the river. They might have
> driven us all out at any time had they been disposed. We often
> heard of attacks that were to be made at certain times, and the
> women became alarmed, but they never came to anything. Most of*

the Indians lived across the river. My brother settled in Columbia township, in 1809 and in going to see him I have rode from the Cuyahoga river twelve miles westward before seeing a house, and that was in Berea. My father bought his land for about one dollar and thirty cents an acre of the Connecticut Land Company. His first house was a log one, and his second, a frame, was built in 1815 in front of the old one some forty rods, and is still standing. Of course the first work of the pioneer was to get his farm cleared as rapidly as possible. The trees were chopped down and the brush burned off. There could be no ploughing among the stumps and roots, and so the surface of the land was merely scratched by a drag. It had to be a stout one with not many teeth, and those large ones. With the surface thus broken, the grain or corn would be put in and do much better than one would suppose. I have seen corn growing in the field while the logs were still there. No drag was used there, but we would "tuck" the corn--that is, make a hole in the ground with some sharp instrument, place the corn therein, and cover it up. We would hoe around it as we could, and keep the weeds cut down.

I have no hunting stories to tell, as I never did a day's hunting in my life. The bears used to be plenty, and they made havoc among the hogs that were allowed to run in the woods to fatten, and occasionally they would even visit the pens near the house. Hogs and cattle were given an ear mark. That mark was recorded in the township book, and each man was thus enabled to claim his own. My father at one time had a flock of twenty-four sheep, and it was my duty as a boy to see that they were shut in their pen each night so the wolves would not get them. One night I forgot them, and in the morning twelve were found dead. Each was torn at the throat, where the wolves drank their blood, but were otherwise uninjured, except one that was torn in the flank. (Mr. Doane, in the article above referred to, gave his recollections of the War of 1812 but the following may be added):

In the panic that swept all through this section after Hull's surrender, when the approach of the Indians and British was falsely announced and everybody was in a panic, one man, named Hawley Tanner, was determined that the enemy should gain no benefit from his growing garden. He accordingly turned his cattle into it, and they made short work of it. When the alarm was seen to be without foundation, Mr. Tanner came back and saw his fine patch in a needless ruin. There were many other incidents of a like character. The first stage coaches commenced to go by about 1810, as nearly as I can remember. They were a great curiosity to me, as I had never seen four horses driven together, nor a carriage of any kind. The first that I knew anything about were owned by Seth Reed, of Erie. They could not make more than forty or fifty miles a day, and sometimes the roads were awful. Passengers had to often alight and pry the coach out of the mud. There was a hill three miles below here that was in an awful condition, and sometimes a yoke of oxen had to be sent to help four horses drag an empty coach up it. It is not much better now. The road along here used to run some rods nearer the ridge, but it was moved down to the present place (the Euclid road) because of the springs that troubled the old highway. We were compelled to go or send to Cleveland for our mails, for a number of years. I remember the excitement consequent on the building of the canal, and when it was opened every one was expected to ride down to Boston and back. The first money I have recollection of was silver, and no one had too much of that. We were compelled to do our trading in coon skins, bear skins, and pearl ash, or black salts. The first school I attended was in Newburgh in 1805. I boarded with a man named Williams, (probably William Wheeler Williams) who built the first grist mill in Newburg, the stones of which are now in possession of the Historical Society. I believe that a daughter of Squire Spafford was our teacher. There were some twenty-five children attended, and there were not enough books in the whole community to give us each an outfit. Afterwards a school was started below us, but I never had much chance in it. It held only three months in the winter and three in the Summer, but the boys were kept so busy hoeing corn and picking up brush that they did not get much of a chance at the summer term. *The first religious meetings held in the township were in 1805 or 1806 in a log building with a large fireplace in one end. People came to service regardless of a little rain or cold. The congregation would run from twenty-five to forty. In 1816 a frame church was built. It at first had no method of heating. On cold days the women would go into the school house that stood near, where a great fire was roaring, fill their foot-stoves with coals, take them into the church, and keep as warm as they could during the services. Rev. Thomas Barr, father of the late Judge Barr, was our first settled pastor. He came in 1811 and remained until 1820 when he went to Wooster. He preached the straight Calvanistic doctrine, and some of it he gave to us quite blue and warm. He was a strong temperance man. In those days whisky was kept in every house, and if one went to a neighbor's and was not offered a drink of whiskey he went away with a poor opinion of his host. It was brought out on all occasions. I raised in 1830 the first barn ever put up in Euclid without whisky. I gave the men cider, coffee, cheese and cake, and they seemed as well satisfied as though their drink had been still stronger. [The barn still stands in good preservation near the Euclid road, a few rods west of Mr. Doan's present dwelling. The siding put on in 1830 was nearly all there, and no paint has ever been put upon it.]*

Of the cholera scare, Mr. Doan said:

I remember that very well. My cousin Job Doan died of it. People were as badly frightened hereabout as they were elsewhere. There was a rumor that an infected ship load was to land at Euclid creek, and a crowd of men got together to go down and prevent them. The story turned out to have no foundation.

Mr. Doane has lived a quiet and useful life, doing well whatever his, hands found to-do, and never endeavoring to make a stir in the world. As a child he was feeble, and as a man he was never very strong, but he worked steadily and did not give up working until two years ago. Since then he has done nothing. He has lived nearly all his life on the same farm, completing his eighty-seventh year upon it in November last. There is not a man or woman liv-

ing in the county who was here when he came. He has seen many
wonderful changes in his day, and had any one told him sixty years
ago of what was to be in the course of his life, he would have set the
prophet down as a crazy dreamer of dreams.

John Doane passed away on October 16, 1896 at his home in Collamer. He, his parents and siblings, children and other extended members of the family reside in Sections 2 and 6.

Timothy Doane, Sr. set the example for his children as he served this country during the American Revolution with his father and brother. The records indicate he served in Capt. George Webb's company, Col. William Shephard's regiment for the town of Eastham, Massachusetts for a term of eight months.[59] The records further indicate that Timothy and his brother Seth were prisoners on the Jersey prison ship in New York in 1776. They were released as part of an exchange with the British and told they would all have a wonderful meal before they were released home. Everyone ate the soup except for Timothy as he did not like onions. All that ate the soup died either on the way home or soon after their arrival home, including Timothy's brother Seth. Seth did make the journey home, but just in time to "lie down and die."[60]

After the war and before his arrival in Cleveland, Timothy was the Master of a ship called the Union. He made regular trips to the West Indies to transport goods and services back to the United States. Of further note is that the Doane family are Mayflower descendents through Timothy's mother Mercy Parker. Mercy was the daughter of John and Elizabeth (nee Smith) Parker of Falmouth. Elizabeth was the daughter of Joseph and Anne (nee Fuller) Smith. Ann was the daughter of Edward Fuller, son of Samuel Fuller of the Mayflower. Samuel and his wife both died their first winter in the United States.

Ebenezer Duty -- Mr. Duty was born June 2, 1782 in Derryfield, New Hampshire. He was married to Sarah, whose father, Moses Warren, was a veteran of the Revolutionary War. Mr. Duty settled in Ashtabula in 1808, while he was preparing the home for his family he became the father of two twin girls, Louisa and Lovisa. Thereafter, Mr. Duty sent for his wife and children who traveled to Ashtabula with her father, brother Daniel and his family. They traveled from Acworth, New Hampshire in a covered wagon which it is reported Sally drove. There was a basket suspended from the top of the wagon which held the 6 week old twin babies.[61]

Mr. Duty was an expert in the making of brick and is reported to have produced the first bricks in Northern Ohio. The bricks made by the family were used to build the Jefferson courthouse and the first Ohio penitentiary in 1813. The first Ohio penitentiary was built *on a ten-acre lot in the southwest corner of Columbus, which was conveyed to the State for that purpose by the original proprietors of the town. It was a brick building fronting on Scioto street; the dimensions were sixty by thirty feet and three stories in height, which included the basement partly below ground. The basement contained the living-rooms of the prisoners and could only be entered from the prison-yard. The second story was the keeper's resident. The third or upper story contained the prisoners' cells, thirteen in number, nine of which were light and four dark cells.*

The prison-yard, about 100 feet square, was enclosed by a stone wall from fifteen to eighteen feet high.[62]

Mr. Duty started a brick making company with his sons Daniel and Andrew. Their company was known by several different names over the years, namely, Duty & Co. (1897); Deckman-Duty Brick Company (1908); and Medal Brick & Tile Company (1916 to 1940). These were the first bricks to be manufactured in the county according to the records of H. L. Morrison. Deckman and Duty was also reported to have produced the first paving brick in the State of Ohio and was the largest of its kind in the State. Mr. Duty was described as an *"astute man and helped to try cases before justices of the peace."*[63]

Mr. Duty passed away on September 7, 1852. He and his family reside in Section 4, Lot 25. The Duty lot is the most beautifully maintained family lot in the cemetery, the family hired a caretaker for their lot.

Edwin Duty – Mr. Duty was born on November 8, 1830 in Waterville, Oneida County, New York the son of Andrew W. and Eliza Duty (Andrew W. being the son of the above mentioned Ebenezer Duty.) Mr. Duty married Naomi Meeker, the daughter of Stephen C. and Elizabeth

EDWIN DUTY.

The Cleveland Leader

(nee Chips) Meeker on November 23, 1852. She passed away on July 16, 1860. He married a second time to Elizabeth Ann (Lizzy) Salter, the daughter of Richard and Harriet Salter on December 2, 1860.

At the age of twenty-two he took charge of the family farm and operated it until 1857. Mr. Duty then began his career as superintendent of Cleveland's street railway system that spanned over 40 years. He remembers the beginning of Cleveland's public transportation system:

> *Superintendent of Construction Edwin Duty, of the Big Consolidated Street Railway Company, to whom old-time residents of Cleveland were indebted for the novelty of riding in street carts drawn through the street by oxen, and whom President Everett, of the Big Consolidated Company, is in the habit of introducing as the father of the street railways of Cleveland, celebrated the fortieth anniversary of his work as a street railway superintendent Wednesday. He celebrated the anniversary by attending to his regular work just as though it was not a milestone in an exceptionally interesting career.*

Superintendent Duty was the superintendent of the first street car line Cleveland had, and after he had been in the position longer than most men remain in one position, he learned the business all over again and mastered the operation of the electric lines the same as he had mastered the running of the horse cars. There is perhaps no man in the county and country with a longer unbroken career as a street railway superintendent. His recollections of the early days of Cleveland's street railway systems are interesting.

"The first street car run in Cleveland, made a trial trip over the first line September 6th, 1860," he said yesterday. "The line was not opened until September 10th, the day that the Perry monument in the Public Square was dedicated and one of the biggest days in Cleveland's early history. The formal opening of the street railway line was almost as great an event in the minds of the citizens as the dedication of the monument. Two separate street railway lines opened that day, and they both carried all the passengers they could accommodate. One of them was the old Kinsman street line, afterward the Woodland avenue line, and the other was the East Cleveland Street Railway Company line, of which I was superin-

East Cleveland Trolley, 1910

tendent, my appointment dated from the day the line was formally opened.

"*The line was called the East Cleveland line because it ran to what was then East Cleveland, that is, to the station of the Cleveland and Pittsburgh Railroad at Euclid avenue, near Willson avenue. Willson avenue was then the city limits on the east. The line was a single track one, and remained a single track line for years. It started from the post office on the Public Square, and ran up Superior street to Case avenue, and the on out Euclid avenue to the railroad station at the corner of Euclid and Willson avenues. The business on the cars was heavy the first day, although I don't remember the number of passengers carried. For the first six months the takings of the road averaged from $25 to $30 per day, and the about of this was in 'construction ticket' as they were called. The road was built with but little cash capitalization. Tickets, each good for one ride on the cars after the line should have been completed, were issued for work on the road. It was six months before these tickets were used up and the income of the company was in cash instead of the construction tickets. Meanwhile the income of the road, as far as actual cash was concerned, was between $12 and $15 per day.*

"*When the road was built, Euclid avenue east of the Square was a much less important business street than Superior street between the Square and Erie street, and that is the reason the tracks went up Superior street to Erie street. The road started with four cars, three of them sixteen feet long and the other fourteen. They carried twenty-two passengers, and it took them twenty-five minutes to make the run from the Square to Willson avenue. Now the time is about fifteen minutes. Two of the cars used at first had seats on top, and in the summer time the passengers used to climb up ladders to these seats, because they could see the city so much better there.*

"*During the civil war it was very hard to get men for the cars, because everybody wanted to go into the army. Another time when* it was very hard to keep the line running was in the early seventies, when an epidemic laid up most of the horses in the city.

"The street car horses all got the disease, and we were told that if they were worked they would die. So we did not take the horses out of the stables for about two weeks.

"We hired all the mules we could, and still did not have enough for all the cars, and then we hired six pairs of oxen. We got them from the members of the Shaker community on the heights back of the city. The owners of the cattle would not trust our drivers with them, and they used to walk along beside the oxen when they were hitched to the cars, and drive them with their long whips. The people thought it was a great joke. It was funny to see a car moving slowly along the street drawn by a pair of big, long-horned oxen, with the Shaker owner walking beside them, and the driver of the car with nothing to do but put on the brakes to stop the car. When the bell rant for the car to stop, the driver of the car would shout to the driver of the oxen, and the latter would shout to his cattle, and then the brakes would be set and the car stopped.

"It was even slower and harder work to get the cars started, for the oxen and their drivers were not used to doing things in a hurry and they never learned to hustle. Of course the oxen would never go faster than a walk, and it used to take an hour to make the trip from Willson avenue to the Square. The public seemed to think it was a good joke, but it was hard on the company because when anyone was in a hurry he would walk.

"When the line was started, cars used to be run every twenty minutes, and this was thought to be excellent service. There was not a paved street in the city in those days, and in muddy weather the cars, horses and drivers used to be so covered with mud that they looked like moving mud heaps.

"There was a lively fight for the right to lay tracks through the lower portion of Euclid avenue, between Erie street and the Square. The fight lasted for weeks, the property owners taking the matter into court and getting an injunction against the company. The street was not paved then, and on the day the case was heard *and the injunction dissolved, I was all ready with a gang of men, and as soon as the court dissolved the injunction I started a plow at the Square and plowed a furrow through the middle of the avenue clear to Erie street, so as to have the work under way before anything more could be done by those who opposed the road. In two days we had the tracks laid and cars were running.*

"Dr Everett, the father of the president of the Big Consolidated was the man who gave to Cleveland its trolley railways. He had seen that the cable system was not the right thing, and had also spent a good deal of money in an experiment with the underground electric idea. He built about a mile of track operated by the underground trolley on Quincy street, but the experiment did not prove a success. My wife ran the first car over that road, and Dr. Everett was on the front platform with her, there being a number of prominent men in the car. Mrs. Duty ran the car faster than Dr. Everett thought was safe, and he kept saying 'Not so fast! Not so fast!' The trip was made without any mishap, but the plan was never adopted, because it was thought to be impossible to prevent the escape of the current from the underground wires.

"It was about 1890 that the motive power was changed from horse to trolley. At that time the company had 700 horses and 200 cars. Some of the cars were changed to motors and others were used for years as trailers. It was Dr. Everett who brought the change about and gave the city one of the finest street transportation systems in the country. He spent a good deal of money investigating before he made the change, and the officers of the company, including myself, went to Richmond, Va., to investigate the trolley systems there.

"The original East Cleveland street car line was built by a contractor named Stone. Since I have been superintendent, I have laid and relaid that line four times, and have had superintendence of all the track laying the Big Consolidated has done since. In all, I must have laid several hundred miles of street car track in Cleveland. While I was superintendent of the old lines I used to have to stay out all night fighting blizzards to keep the tracks clear, so that

the line would not be tied up, and there have been times when it was impossible to keep the cars running. We used to have a number of big bob-sleds that we would run during the winter when the snow was so deep that we could not sue the cars. There are some of those old bob-sleds around in some of the company's barns yet. There were no sweepers and snow plows, such as we have now, in those days, and it used to be very hard to keep the lines open all winter."64

Mr. Duty, his two wives and other members of his family reside in Section 8, Lot 35.

Edwards Family – Adonijah Edwards was born in 1740 in Coventry, Connecticut. He married Mary (Polly) Searles in 1765 in Coventry who was born in approximately 1732. Adonijah and Polly arrived in Cleveland with their eldest son Roldolphus. Adonijah is a veteran of the Revolutionary War having served as a Private in the Vermont Line.

Roldolphus was born on January 26, 1759 in Tolland County, Connecticut. Mr. Edwards served in 1790 as a Private in the Indian War in Captain Strong's Company. In 1794 Rodolphus was a surveyor in Otsego County, New York and in 1796 thru 1797 worked as a merchant in Herkimer County, New York. In 1798 Rodolphus and his family along with the family of Nathaniel Doan departed for Cleveland. He settled for a brief time in the Black River country (Lorain County). On June 10, 1798 he arrived in Cleveland in an oxen boat with his two brothers Rufus and Ebenezer.

Rodolphus planted a small potato patch along the river bank near the fork of Superior Street in Cleveland and moved to the ridge that became Newburgh in October, 1798 where he built a log cabin. Elijah Gunn, Nathaniel Doan, James Kingsbury, Ezekial Hawley, R. H. Blinn and James Hamilton were his neighbors. A life long animosity apparently existed between Rodolphus and James Kingsbury, the details of which are unknown.

On April 5, 1802 Rodolphus Edwards was elected chairman of Cleveland at the first town meeting held at James Kingsbury's house.

In 1803 he was Clerk of Elections and from 1815 to 1818 he served as Justice of the Peace.[65]

Rodolphus Edwards, for short called "Dolph" and of whom I am about to write, can be numbered among the early pioneers of Cuyahoga county, having come here away back in 1797. He settled on a large tract of land now known as Woodland Hills, but formerly called Butternut Ridge. In addition to farming he kept a public inn or tavern, as they were called in those days, for the accommodation of the traveling public, which was a place of resort for the old pioneers who used to occasionally meet and over their glasses of cider-flip and pass away the time recounting their trials and adventures of pioneer life. This old house is still standing, having been converted into a private residence, and is now occupied by Rodolphus Edwards., Jr., who himself is well advanced in years. Rain or snow, hot or cold, as regular as Saturday came around Uncle Dolph, with his old Dobbin, old time carryall and big brindle dog, seated bolt upright on the seat by the side of his master, would make his appearance in town. He would drive up to a post in front of a certain store, and after hitching his horse he would gather up his jugs which were to be filled with molasses, vinegar and certain other liquids for the benefit of his traveling customers, he would at once attend to having them filled and making purchases of such other articles as he desired, and having safely stowed them away in his wagon would leave his faithful dog on guard while he visited his numerous friends and whiled away the day in talking over old times. When ready to return home it would sometimes happen, especially in very hot weather, that by the time he would get comfortably seated in his carryall he would become somewhat drowsy and drop into a doze, and the lines would hang listlessly in his hands, but Old Dobbin would trot off homewards all the same, while Old Brindle would sit as solemn as a judge and keep faithful vigil over both master and horse, until all were safely landed at the Edward's mansion. Rodolphus Edwards has long since finished life's journey, and but few of the old pioneers now remain.[66]

S. J. Kelly documents the story of Rodolphus *"who made his home side-by-side with Lorenzo Carter"* in a *Cleveland Plain Dealer* article titled *"Rodolphus Edwards – Cleveland's Unofficial Mayor."*

> *In the meantime in 1802 the Quarter Sessions Court ordered the first town meeting for the election of trustees, appraisers and supervisors for the township of Cleveland, held at the house of Judge Kingsbury. It was held April 5, and Rodolphus Edwards was made chairman. The rest of the seventeen officials were chose from township clerk, lister, and overseers of the poor, down to constables and "fence viewers."*
>
> *The election of Edwards as chairman of the trustees made him the first "unofficial" mayor of Cleveland. His chairmanship gave him the same position as that of a mayor over the mapped-out "City of Cleveland" and the whole township.*
>
> *The humorous side of his holding the highest office position over Cleveland is that he never lived within the city limits. His first cabin was built just south of Superior Street Hill and all that land on the river bank was outside the boundaries of the town of that time.*[67]

Rodolphus' son, Rodolphus passed away in 1890. Upon his passing the Early Settlers Association remembered him as well as his father. The younger Rodolphus is not buried in East Cleveland Township Cemetery. Yet the following documents further the life of Rodolphus, Sr. and his family:

> *Rodolphus Edwards, whose death occurred at his home on Woodland Hills, on Thursday, August 21, 1890 was a son of Rodolphus Edwards. The latter was a member of the surveying party in the Western Reserve in 1798, in which year he arrived at Cleveland, together with Nathaniel Doan, wife, one son and three daughters, Samuel Dodge, father of the late Henry Dodge, Nathan Chapman, Stephen Gilbert and Joseph Landon. These eleven persons were the total permanent additions to the population of*

Cleveland during the year 1798. Mr. Edwards had followed surveying previous to coming here, and the compass used by him from 1792 to 1798 may be seen in the rooms of the Historical Society, to which it was donated by Mr. Edwards, recently deceased. Mr. Edwards, Sr., the first year he was in Cleveland built a log cabin "under the hill" at the foot of Superior street. He remained there, however, but a short time, and on account of the malaria at the mouth of the Cuyahoga, removed in a year or two, with two or three other families, to the high land running from Doan's Corners to Newburg. He appears to have been a man of much intelligence and great good sense and judgment, and was very useful in the early days of the Reserve. He was chairman of the first town meeting held in Cleveland, April 5, 1802, at the house of James Kingsbury. Mr. Edwards came here from Chenango county, New York, but the family is of Connecticut origin, the father of Rodolphus, Sr., having been born in Tolland county, in that State, in 1739. Later he also came to Cleveland, and died at the house of his son, in 1831 aged ninety-two years. His name was Adonijah. He was in the war of the Revolution under General Stark, who as he drew his forces up to attack Burgoyne, said to his men: "Fellow-soldiers, there is the enemy. If we do not take them Molly Stark will be a widow to-night." Rodolphus Edwards, Sr., heard from the lips of his father much of the history of that great war for the independence of this country, as well as the part taken in it by his father, and in memory of the gallant and brave general under whom his father served, named his first son Stark, who was born December 6 1808, and died June 19 1877.[68]

Mr. Edwards is credited with surveying the first road from the Pennsylvania line to Cleveland in 1798. The compass he used is reported to be in the Western Reserve Historical Society Museum.[69] Mr. Edwards passed away on July 7, 1840, his parents and other family members are buried in Section 12, Lots 3 and 5.

Fogel Family – It would seem remiss not include some biographical information regarding the people that were the reason for that maiden journey to East Cleveland Township Cemetery. Gustaf and Carl, brothers who shared the same father but had different mothers, immigrated to the United States from Rejmyre, Skedevi Parish, Östergötland län, Sweden in 1885 and 1888 respectively. All the siblings were born with the surname of Flinta and utilized that surname while in Sweden. Gustaf was given the surname Fogel, while serving his mandatory service in the military prior to leaving Sweden. Many of the siblings who actually arrived in the Unites States prior to Gustaf took the name Fogel upon arrival, only two of the six siblings that immigrated continued to use the surname Flinta.

They were glassworkers at the Reijmyre Glasbruk in their hometown. The immigration was prompted by two of the brothers being recruited to a glass factory in Braddock, Pennsylvania. Shortly after arrival in Braddock, the glass factory closed and the families slowly moved farther west to Cleveland. The family attended the First Swedish Baptist Church which was located at Wade Park and Addison for many years. Many of the Fogel/Flinta family continue to live in the Cleveland area today.

Gustaf and his wife, Anna Mathilda reside in Section 8, Lot 110; Carl and his wife Emma reside in Section 2, Lot 78.

Anna Mathilda Fogel, Diane Hamlett VandenBergh Collection

Ford Family -- One of the notable families represented in East Cleveland Township Cemetery is the Ford family that originated in Weymouth, England, with their surname being spelled Foorde. Hezekiah Ford, IV was born on December 29, 1759 in Abington, Plymouth County, Massachusetts and married Huldah Cobb. Huldah passed away on September 11, 1835 in Cummington, Hampshire County, Massachusetts. Hezekiah is a veteran of the Revolutionary War. He participated in the Battle of Bennington, serving as a Private in Captain William Ward's Company of Ezra May's Regiment; served as a Private in Captain Benjamin Booney's Company of Col. Elisha Porter's Hampshire County Regiment; served in New London Connecticut in repelling the attacks of General Arnold, after his treachery; and ultimately served as a Captain in Col. Elisha Porter's Regiment..

Hezekiah and four of his sons became Ohio pioneers in approximately 1837. Hezekiah and three of his sons, namely, Darius, Cyrus and Lewis remained in the Cleveland area with son Ansel moving to Fulton County, Ohio. Cyrus and his son Horatio came in a sleigh from Massachusetts to Ohio. The family's first endeavor was in Massillon, Ohio with an attempt to raise silkworms and mulberries. The family was struck with malaria and decided to move to Cleveland in approximately 1841. Cyrus purchased two farms of approximately 100 acres each, one on Euclid Avenue for approximately $18 per acre and the other on Mayfield Road at approximately $16 per acre.

Cyrus attempted again to raise silkworms and hatched 1,500,000, but never succeeded in getting a cocoon. The reason for the lack of success was attributed to the Ohio climate. At one time he had devoted 18 acres to watermelons. In 1852 Cyrus gave the farm to his son Horace. Horace worked on the farm in the summer months and taught school in the winters.

The Ford family was known for their progressive faming methods. The acres of land purchased soon became orchards of fruit and gardens of vegetables and flowers. It has been said that there was nothing Cyrus was afraid to try and most of his experiments in farming were successful.

The Fords had very strong anti-slavery views. This was a family that did not just talk-the-talk but walked it, with their homes becoming stations of the "Underground Railroad". Cyrus Ford worked closely with Samuel Cozad, III, assisting slaves in escaping to Canada. A following story is told:

> *A beautiful Kentucky girl and a little boy, both so nearly white as to easily pass for such. They had been sold to a cruel New Orleans planter and fled north into Ohio, being passed on from one anti-slavery family to another until they reached the shores of Lake Erie and were received and secreted in the home of Cyrus Ford. A little steamer was then plying between Cleveland and Port Stanley, but its dock was being closely watched by emissaries of the southern master. The woman was dressed in rich apparel, her little boy disguised as a girl, and they were driven in a fine turnout to the boat, and those watching out little guessed that the elegantly attired lady who walked over the gangplank was the poor woman they had planned to seize and return to slavery.*[70]

The Ford women were also very involved in the community. An example is that of Clarissa Whitmarsh Ford, wife of Cyrus. Clarissa was the daughter of Deacon Jacob and Anna Poole Whitmarsh. She was described as "*a woman who could do her own thinking, arrive at her own conclusions, and give her reasons for them with logical clearness.*"

The descendants of Hezekiah Ford continue to be prominent citizens in the Cleveland area today. Not only have they been successful in their business pursuits but also continued to support the communities in which they live.

The Ford family members buried in East Cleveland Township Cemetery, are resting in Section 2, Lots 17, 18, 41, 42, and 43, which are located on the right side of the road as you drive into the cemetery just before the road turns to your right.

Hezekiah received a new headstone on or about October 19, 1941 that was presented by the Sons of the American Revolution. This marker was designed by the Ford family, as described in correspondence of Horatio Ford dated June 14, 1941.

Anna Magdalena Gillett– The most photographed monument in the cemetery belongs to Mrs. Gillett. She was born in 1825 in Baden, and was married to Christopher Gillett who was born in England. From the census records it does not appear that they had any children; they lived in Euclid for a short time, thereafter moving to East Cleveland. It is obvious that she was greatly loved by her husband, based on the monument he erected in her memory.

Author Photograph Collection

John Gould (original subscriber in the Publick Burying Ground) was living in East Cleveland according to the 1860 census with his wife Catherine (nee Hope). He was listed as being 79 years of age and having been born in New Jersey. His occupation was listed as farmer.

There were four members of the Gould family who were transferred from the Publick Burying Ground to East Cleveland Township Cemetery on March 25, 1864, namely, Caroline, Eleanor, George, Philinda (first wife of John) and Worthy. All are buried in Section 6, Lot 36.

Ezra Graves (original subscriber of the Publick Burying Ground) was a pioneer physician in Cleveland. He was born in Albany, New York in approximately 1780, he was married to Sophronia (Sophia) (nee Curtiss) in 1803. The information available indicates that he lived where the Adelbert and Case Colleges stood and that his practice was generally centered on the pioneers living east of Willson Avenue (now East 55th Street). He was described as being eccentric, but a very skilled physician. Their children were Hiram, Deborah and Temperance. Mr. Graves died in 1830, however, his final resting place is unknown.

Lucien Gunn– Mr. Gunn was born on April 23, 1816 in Medina, Ohio, the son of Horace and Anna (nee Pritchard) Gunn. Horace was the son of Elijah Gunn, who was with the original surveying party that headed to the Western Reserve in 1796 under the command of Moses Cleaveland. During the first year of surveying Elijah, his wife and children remained in Conneaut, Ohio where they were in charge of the company's supplies, called *"Castle Stow"*. The surveying party would periodically make trips back to Conneaut to replenish their supplies and then return to Cleveland. In the spring of 1797, the Gunn family left Conneaut bound for Cleveland after *"suffering almost incredible hardships and privations and barely escaping starvation."*[71] In 1808 *"a trail was blazed from Massillon to Wooster and that same year Horace Gunn carried the first mail in the Western Reserve west of Cleveland from Cleveland to Maumee."*[72]

Lucien's father brought him to Cleveland at the age of 14. The following is the story of that arrival:

> On passing through the ground that is now the site of Cleveland, his father turned his oxen into a ten-acre lot that is now the public square. Purchasing thirty acres of the Coit tract, upon which his son, Marcus now resides, he settled there and continues as a resident the remainder of his days.

Lucien was a charcoal-burner for the railroad and was also a farmer. He married Charlotte O. Smith. His life came to a tragic end when he was run over by railroad cars on October 31, 1891. Mr. Gunn and his wife Charlotte O. (nee Smith) rest in Section 9, Lot 62.

Rev. Amos S. Hayden –

Born in Ohio in 1813, came to the Western Reserve in 1835 and died September 10, 1880. Rev. A.S. Hayden was, for nearly fifty years, an active and efficient minister in the ministry of the Disciple Church. He was also a composer of music, and was one of the committee which compiled the Christian Hymn-book, now used by that denomination; and to him, perhaps, more than to any other, is that body of Christians indebted, not only for its church music, but also for his latest work, the "History of the Disciples of the Western Reserve."

In 1850 he was chosen Principal of the Western Reserve Eclectic Institute (now Hiram College), and this position he filled honorably for seven years; since which time he has filled honorable offices in that church, and left an impress upon those among whom he labored that will not soon be forgotten.[73]

Rev. Hayden, his wife Sarah and other family members reside in Section 1, Lot 10.

Aaron Hubbard (original subscriber of the Publick Burying Ground) was born in 1758 and was living in Newburg with his wife according to the 1840 census. His wife, Esther was born in Connecticut. Their son Israel Hubbard and his wife, Rhoda (nee Hulbert), had moved to Newburg and in 1820 Aaron and Esther followed them to Newburgh from Broome, Schoracic County, New York. They lived in a log cabin on the north side of Woodland Avenue reportedly nearly opposite Herald Street. Aaron Hubbard passed away in 1843. It is believed that he was originally buried in the Publick Burying Ground and then transferred to Woodland Cemetery. He and Esther are buried in Section 5, Lot 8 along with other family members.

William H. Hudson (original subscriber of the Publick Burying Ground) was born in 1787 in Massachusetts. The exact time of his arrival in Cleveland is unknown; however, he was living in the Cleveland area in 1819 when he married Delphia Sherwin. Delphia was the daughter of American Revolutionary veteran Ahimaaz Sherwin, Sr. and Ruth Day Sherwin. The 1860 census indicates Mr. Hudson was a gardener by trade and lived in East Cleveland. There are many members of the Hudson family buried in East Cleveland Township Cemetery in Sections 2 and 9. Mr. Hudson and his wife, Delphia Sherwin Hudson are buried in Section 9, Lot 1.

Elijah Ingersoll w(original subscriber of the Publick Burying Ground) as born in approximately 1766 in Massachusetts. Prior to his arrival in Cleveland he married Polly (may have also used the name Mary) Barlow and had nine children. Polly passed away in 1807 and is buried in Massachusetts. Elijah married a second time to Betsey Thomas who accompanied Elijah and the children to Cleveland. Betsey Ingersoll passed away four years after her arrival in Cleveland in approximately 1812. After Betsey's death, Elijah married Rosanna Churchill Parker.

In 1812 Mr. Ingersoll purchased 900 acres of land in Newburgh from the Connecticut Land Company. He passed away in 1834 at 79 years of age; it is believed that he was originally buried in the Publick Burying Ground and removed to East Cleveland Township Cemetery. Elijah, Rosanna and Betsey along with several other family members are buried in Section 5, Lot 5. The monument has toppled, however, the names are still readable.

Nathan Ingersoll (original subscriber of the Publick Burying Ground) was born in 1791 in Lee, Massachusetts the son of Elijah and Polly Ingersoll who is noted above. He married Polly (may have used the name Mary) Perry in 1812 just prior to their journey to Cleveland. According to the 1850 census, Nathan and Polly Ingersoll are listed as living in East Cleveland; no occupation was listed. Mrs. Ingersoll was described as being a woman of great character, always willing to do what was necessary to take care of the less fortunate. On her 90th birthday a story is told of the party she gave for her family and made the cake herself. One can only imagine the size of the party, as Nathan and Polly had seven children all of which were married except for one. More than likely the party included grandchildren and great-grandchildren alike.

The day after the party, Polly walked a mile to the house of relative and later that evening milked their cow.

Polly passed away on April 21, 1880 and is buried next to Nathan in the East Cleveland Township Cemetery, Section 1, Lot 20. Nathan and a large number of the Ingersoll family can be located in Section 1, Lots 19 and 20 of East Cleveland Township Cemetery.

Amos Kingsbury (original subscriber in the Publick Burying Ground) was born July 13, 1793 in New Hampshire and married Clarissa Ingersoll, the daughter of Elijah and Polly Barlow Ingersoll, in 1815 prior to coming to Cleveland. Mr. Kingsbury is the son of Judge James Kingsbury. Judge Kingsbury was one of the original settlers of Cleveland having received 100 acres of land from the Connecticut Land Company, despite the fact he had no connection to the company. Documentation indicates that Mr. Kingsbury had married again by 1820 to Mary Sherman. His death is noted as being January 19, 1858, the location is unknown.

Lee Family –Elias Lee was born in approximately 1760 and arrived in Ohio in 1811 with his wife Mary (may also have been known as Laura – nee Bryan) and at least two sons, Guy and Rowland. Elias was the son of Captain Benjamin Lee who served in the French War. [74] Mary was born in 1755 in New Marlborough, Massachusetts the daughter of Reuben and Mary Bryan. On March 3, 1814 Elias was appointed for a 7 year term as Judge of the Court of Common Pleas in Euclid. After fulfilling this roll for the appointed term he was elected to the House of Representatives for Cuyahoga County for the 1822-1823 term.

Prior to his arrival in Cleveland he served our country during the American Revolution in the Massachusetts Militia. Records indicate he was a Private in Captain Nathan Rowlee's co., Lieut. Col. Timothy Robinson's detachment of Hampshire County militia and indicates he served 83 days at Ticonderoga.[75] Elias passed away on January 28, 1832 and Mary passed away on January 29, 1832 both of typhoid fever. It has been reported that Mary was very devoted to her husband and they had a very strong and happy marriage. It was her final wish that if one of them passed away the other would also go too. They were both buried in the same grave originally in the Publick Burying Ground and thereafter moved to East Cleveland Township Cemetery with his son's (Rowland) family in Section 1, Lot 16. Their obituary in the *Cleveland Herald* read as follows:

> *At his residence in Euclid, on the 28th ult. the Hon. Elias Lee; and on the 29th, his affectionate wife. Mr. Le was a very worthy, respectable, and valuable citizen, and whose loss is met with deep regret, throughout the great circle of his acquaintance. He has ever maintained a steady and unbroken mind, and was greatly attached to the civil and religious freedom of his country. He was a Colonel in the Massachusetts line, where he, no doubt, like of our revolutionary soldiers experienced prosperity and adversity; after which time he located himself at the above named place; where, by an unanimous vote he was elected Judge of the county court. In all the office he has filled, he has received the applause and approbation of all who knew him. He has now, with his beloved wife, departed this life, at the good old age of 72 years. They were interred on the following Monday, in Cleaveland township, near J. Doan's, at which time was delivered a short discourse by Mr. A. Sherwin, accompanied by a large concourse of the citizens of Euclid and Cleaveland.*[76]

Their son Rowland was born in 1805 in Roxbury, Massachusetts. He originally purchased the lot in the Publick Burying Ground and thereafter the lot in the East Cleveland Township Cemetery on February 27, 1862. Elias' Last Will and Testament names Rowland as the Executor.

Andrew Logan (original subscriber in the Publick Burying Ground) was born in approximately 1797 in Beaver, Pennsylvania and arrived in Cleveland prior to 1818. In 1818 Mr. Logan started the first newspaper in Cleveland called the *Cleveland Gazette and Commercial Register*. The first publication was issued on July 31, 1818. The newspaper office was located on the southwest corner of Public Square and Superior where Marshall's Drug Store once stood. The one-story building measured 10 X 20 feet. The newspaper survived only fifteen months ceasing operations in 1819 which was the same time the *Cleveland Herald* came into existence.[77] After the closure of the newspaper, Mr. Logan became the first inspector of Cleveland and operated the hay scales.

Mr. Logan married Phila Sherwin in 1820, the daughter of Ahimaaz Sherwin, Sr. and Ruth Day Sherwin. Andrew and Phila remained in Cleveland until at least 1840 when a son James was born. The 1850 and 1860 census indicates Andrew and Phila are living in Iowa along with children Joseph, Sherwin, Olivia, Jackson and Martin. Sherwin Logan apparently returned to Cleveland at some point and married his cousin Caroline, the daughter of Ahimaaz Sherwin, Jr. There is some indication that Andrew became the editor of the *Davenport Iowa News*. The census information indicates he was a farmer. Caroline Logan is buried in the Sherwin family plots in East Cleveland Township Cemetery, Section 8, Lot 30.

Humphrey Nichols (original subscriber in the Publick Burying Ground) was born in approximately 1789 in New Hampshire. He married Mariah Bunce in 1824. He is listed as a farmer in the 1850 census living in East Cleveland. The family reports that the City of Cleveland took possession of quite a bit of Nichols' land under eminent domain, for Rockefeller Park prior to 1920. They also report that the original Nichols' cabin was located on the site of the former Mt. Sinai Hospital.

To make things interesting for family historians, Humphrey and Mariah named a son Jesse (b. 1826 – d. 1916), who in turn had a son Jesse (b. 1865 – d. 1950) both of whom are buried in East Cleveland Township Cemetery, Section 7, Lot 37. Humphrey also had a brother named Jesse.

Records indicate Humphrey passed away in October 1868 at the age of 79 and was buried in Woodland Cemetery, Section 31, Lot 18.

Jesse Nichols (original subscriber in the Publick Burying Ground) was born in 1798 and it is believed came to Cleveland from Weare, New Hampshire, probably with his brother Humphrey Nichols in 1815. Jesse passed away in 1823 and it is believed he was originally buried in the Publick Burying Ground and then transferred to Woodland Cemetery on April 20, 1870. He is buried in Section 31, Lot 18 along with his brother Humphrey.

Jesse and Humphrey's father, Humphrey Nichols, was born in 1755 in Aesbury, Essex County, Massachusetts. He served in the American Revolution, after which he moved to Weare, New Hampshire and had 13 children. Humphrey, Sr. worked as either a blacksmith or silversmith, then as a dairy farmer. He passed away in 1839.

Ransom O'Connor –

Born in Ohio 1824, came to the Western Reserve in 1824, died May 7, 1882. Ransom O'Connor was a thriving farmer, and for many years an active member of the Disciple Church in Collamer."[78]

Mr. O'Connor and his family are buried in Section 1, Lots 24, 25, 26, 27 and 28.

Charles E. Reader – Mr. Reader was born in 1844 the son of James and Cynthia Reader. He was a veteran of the Civil War having served in Company K, 195th Infantry Regiment; he was mustered out on 18 December 1865 in Washington, DC. He married Emily (nee Rand) the daughter of Charles and Rachel Rand. There were at least three children born of the marriage, Emily, Edward and Melvin. The 1900 census documents that Mr. Reader was working at the stone quarries. Mr. Reader passed away on or about November 30, 1909 at the Soldiers and Sailors Home.

It is said that Mr. Reader arranged to have the dog that was so faithfully guarding his grave sculpted prior to his death. Neighbors surrounding the cemetery have reported they would look out the back windows of their homes and see the dog. The dog wandered off sometime around the 1980s or later. Perhaps if you see this dog you could guide him back home to Section 9, Lot 48 to continue to watch over the family.

Cleveland Press Collection, Cleveland State University

Rev. Peter Ritter – Rev. Ritter was born March 28, 1837 in Bavaria, Germany the son of George and Mary Ann (nee Grindling) Ritter. At the age of seventeen he departed Germany bound for America. He worked on a farm for several years after his arrival in the America; and then attended the theological seminary at Rochester, New York from 1864 to 1867.

Rev. Ritter arrived in Cleveland in 1892 after being elected to a position with the General Conference of the German Baptist Churches. This organization published *Der Sendbote* (The Messenger) for German-American Baptists. It was the prime source for information regarding the German Baptist Conference (now the North American Baptist General Conference). At its founding it was one of only ten German language religious newspapers in the country. *Der Sendbote* was originally published in Cincinnati but was relocated to Cleveland in 1869.[79]

Rev. Ritter married his first wife in 1857, Mary Maurer, in Morganville, New York. She passed away in September, 1891. The second wife was Clara Maef, who was a graduate of the Ladies Seminary at Le

Roy, New York. Rev. and Mrs. (Clara) Ritter reside in Section 12, Lot 79 along with their children Calvin P. and Paul.

John Sherman (original subscriber of the Publick Burying Ground) was born in 1775 in New York. It is unclear when he and his wife arrived in Cleveland. Based on the burial information John's wife was named Electa. They were transferred from the Publick Burying Ground to East Cleveland Township Cemetery. In the 1850 census John is listed as living in East Cleveland Township with an occupation of farmer. John and Electa reside in Section 9, Lot 19.

Ahimaaz Sherwin, Sr. (original subscriber in the Publick Burying Ground) was born in 1759 in Boxford, Essex County, Massachusetts and was a veteran of the American Revolution. In August of 1818, his son Ahimaaz, Jr. returned from Cleveland to lead Ahimaaz, Sr. and Ruth Day Sherwin, his mother, to the new homestead. Ahimaaz and Ruth traveled by horse and wagon from Vermont to Buffalo. At this point in the trip they separated from their son and other children who continued the trip via Lake Erie.

Ahimaaz, Sr. passed away on December 31, 1839, the following obituary was in the *Cleveland Herald* on January 6, 1840:

> ***Another Revolutionary Soldier Gone.*** *Died on the 31st ult., at his residence in Cleveland township, near Doan's Corners., Mr. Ahimaaz Sherwin, father of our respected citizen of the same name, in the 81st year of his age. He was a soldier of the revolution, and lived to see the experiment of self government prove itself superior to every other system, for the protection of human rights and the promotion of human happiness.*
>
> *He felt a deep interest in the prosperity of his country, and had entire confidence in its political institutions. He lived a life of rectitude, and when the infirmities of old age embittered his enjoyments, he looked calmly forward to his approaching dissolution, as the end of all his afflictions. He was not a sectarian. Like a shock of corn fully ripe, he was gathered to his fathers in peace. May the living remember and imitate his virtues.*

A life of virtue leaves a blaze of light,
To mark the path of such as will do right,
Let all like him pursue the path of peace,
And do good deeds till time with us shall cease.

Ahimaaz, Sr. was originally buried in the Publick Burying Ground with his wife, Ruth Day Sherwin. They were removed from the Publick Burying Ground to the East Cleveland Township Cemetery. Ruth Day Sherwin passed away on May 19, 1833, her obituary as it was recorded in the *Cleveland Herald* on May 25, 1833 read as follows:

Died in this town, on the 19th inst. Mrs. Ruth Sherwin, wife of Ahimaaz Sherwin, Esq. in the 74th year of her age.
Blessed are the dead who die in the Lord.

In April 1907 Ahimaaz Sherwin, Sr. was removed to Lake View Cemetery. The records indicate that the balance of the family remain in East Cleveland Township Cemetery.

Ahimaaz Sherwin, Jr. (original subscriber in the Publick Burying Ground) was born in 1792 in Vermont. In February 1818 Ahimaaz, Jr. along with his wife Hannah Swan Sherwin and daughter Lucy boarded a large sleigh drawn by two farm horses in route for Cleveland. The trip took approximately 18 days as travel was made easier by the snow, despite the harsh weather. Upon arrival in Cleveland they took refuge at Job Doan's tavern.

Ahimaaz, Jr. eventually purchased 15 acres from Judge John H. Strong on the corner of Euclid Avenue and East 96th Street. On August 29, 1846 he is credited with organizing the Cuyahoga County Anti-Horse Stealing Club. The census records for 1850 and 1860 indicate his occupation was a farmer, records indicate he was also a very skilled carpenter working in many of the homes and hotels within the Cleveland area. Ahimaaz, Jr. died in 1881 at the age of 89 years, he and many of his family reside in Lake View Cemetery, Section 1, Lot 9.

Horatio Slade – Mr. Slade was born in September 1827 the son of Edward W. and Mary Slade. The family arrived in the United States on

July 7, 1834 on the ship Barque Woodman which sailed from Bristol, Great Britain. He married Elizabeth Camp in 1852. In the 1850 census their occupation is listed as farmer.

> *Mr. Horatio Slade was born in England in 1827, came to Cleveland 1834, died 1882. Mr. Slade was at the time of his death a member of the Disciples' Church of Collamer and one of its Trustees.*[80]

Mr. Slade, along with other his wife Elizabeth and sons Horatio B. and Howard reside in Section 13, Lot 50. The markers on the lot are all illegible. His parents Edward W. and Mary reside in Section 2, Lot 7.

Samuel Spangler (original subscriber in the Publick Burying Ground) was born April 15, 1790, the son of Michael and Catherine (nee Schweissguth) Spangler of Paradise Township, York County, Pennsylvania. His parents would send three sons, Michael, Samuel and Benjamin, to the wilderness that was the newly formed State of Ohio. Samuel was in Cleveland as early as December 24, 1821 for the birth of his daughter, Elizabeth. He is listed as living in Cleveland beginning with the 1830 census, with his occupation listed as a farmer in the census record. According to the family, Samuel's family was the first "German speaking" family in Cuyahoga County.

Samuel's brother Michael served in the War of 1812 as a private under Captain William Albans' Company, 2nd Regiment Ohio Militia. Michael purchased the Commercial Coffee House that was located on lot 54 at the northwest corner of Superior and Seneca (now West 3rd Street). The Commercial Coffee House was later renamed Spangler's Tavern. Brother Benjamin lived in Stark County, Ohio and remained there until his death in 1876.

Samuel Spangler married Catherine Neff, daughter of Johan Peter and Susanna (nee Blasser) Neff, at Christ Lutheran Church in York, Pennsylvania in 1811. The couple had eleven children, several who remained in the Cleveland area. Samuel owned property east of the Dunham Tavern on a part of Lot 338. He was appointed a road overseer and East 73rd Street was once known as Spangler Avenue.

Daughter Louisa married John Dorsh they had two children that died in infancy and were buried in the Publick Burying Ground along with Louisa's sister Eliza. The children were all removed to East Cleveland Township Cemetery in 1860 and can be found in Section 8, Lot 14, along with Samuel, Catherine and Louisa.

James Strong (original subscriber in the Publick Burying Ground) was born in 1784 in Connecticut, the son of John Harris and Elizabeth (nee Cary) Strong. John Harris Strong was a Common Pleas Court Judge from 1817 until his death in 1823. Judge Strong owned the land on the South side of Euclid from East 79th Street to East 107th Street. James was their eldest son. His first wife was Anna Eliza Baldwin, the daughter of Seth Cogswell Baldwin and Ruth White Baldwin. Anna Eliza died eight years after their marriage leaving two children, James H. and Ann Olivia Strong. James married a second time to Erastus Carter Miles, who was the daughter of Lorenzo Carter (the first reported settler in Cleveland). James was one of the early Sheriffs of Cuyahoga County.

Henry/Harvey Sumner (original subscriber in the Publick Burying Ground) is a bit of a mystery. What is known is that he married Sarah Sherwin who was born in 1783 the daughter of Ahimaaz, Sr. and Ruth Day Sherwin. Sarah passed away on September 30, 1827. No record could be found of Henry/Harvey in the census records after the death of his wife.

Teare Family – William H. and Thomas R. Teare the sons of John C. and Catherine (nee Shimmon) Teare were both born in Warrensville after their parents emigrated from the Isle of Man. The Isle of Man is located in the Irish Sea, between England, Scotland, Northern Ireland and Wales. It is considered a strongly independent island that has the oldest continuous parliament in the world, Tynwald.

The Manx early settlers of Cleveland were remembered in the following *Cleveland Leader* article published on July 22, 1896:

> *From the little isle of Man came one of the most valuable ingredients of Cleveland's population. it was a contribution of people which began in the village period.*

The number of Manxmen in and near Cleveland is estimated at several thousand. The proportion of the entire population of the city is not large but it constitutes a quota as decided in its effects as it has been beneficial. They were noteworthy for the readiness with which they became identified with the interests and the order of their new home, rooting themselves quickly and firmly in the land to give more than they should draw from it. They were industrious, intelligent, and strictly temperate.

Manx immigration began in the third decade of Cleveland history, while the place was yet a village of a few hundred people, and has been continued to the present. The honour of being the first Manxman to visit Cleveland lies between Dr. Harrison and Kelly Gawne, and the latter was at least the first to remain. He was with the British army in the war of 1812 and through some connection with a duel while the army was at New Orleans he had occasion to come northward individually and reacted Cleveland. Dr. Harrison was a surgeon in the British navy and traveled extensively about the world. In one of his trips prior to 1820, he stopped at the mouth of the Cuyahoga, and was greatly impressed with its future prospects by reason of its environment and strategic situation. His accounts of the locality on his return directed attention to it as a desirable goal for emigration and in 1824 one family came out, by mistake settling in Painesville. William Kelly and his family, in 1826, came on and settled in Newburg township and he was shortly followed by William Caine. in the years 1827 and 1828 over a hundred families settled about what is now the "South End", more particularly from Union Street southward. It came to he true that one could pass for five or six miles in a line through Newburg township and have Manx farms on either hand all the way. Among those who came with the movement of 1827 were the families of Mr. Kerruish. Rev. Thomas Corlett, and Thomas Quayle, the latter one of the names most prominently connected with the development of the Lake merchant marine.

The Manx people of Cleveland were mostly Methodists in their denominational following and in the early days public services were *held in the Gaelic language near Warrensville. One of the earliest preachers was a Methodist minister - Pastor Cannell - who exercised great influence and who held services in his own log house and later led in having a church edifice erected on the Corlett farm. He was seventy three years old when he came to America A large proportion of the membership of the old Wesleyan Methodist Church which existed on Euclid Avenue years ago, were Manx people, and many of them are members of the First Methodist Church.*

A relief society has been in existence among the Cleveland Manxmen for the past forty-five years and some years ago possessed a literary department. Another organization is Mona's Mutual Benefit Society. Some of the representative Manxmen of Cleveland, besides those mentioned, are W.S. Kerruish, a prominent attorney, James Christian, once a superintendent of the infirmary, and well known as a local preacher; John Gill, a member of the Ohio Legislature; the late Judge Sherwood, M.G. Watterson, once county treasurer the late T.J. Carran, a member of the Ohio Senate; and W.R. Radcliffe, well known before his death for connection in various capacities with the city government.

Thomas R. and his wife Eliza and son Allen Clarke; William H., his wife Margaret and daughter Olive all reside in Section 2, Lots 23 and 24. William H. Teare was remembered by the Early Settlers Association at the time of his passing:

William H. Teare died suddenly September 29, 1911, aged 61 years. He was born in Warrensville, Jan. 15, 1850, the second in the family of nine children. His parents were pioneer Manx settlers in Cuyahoga County, having located in Warrensville in 1836. Mr. Teare is survived by his mother, Mrs. Catherine Teare, who is now 93 years old and by two brothers, John C. Teare of Warrensville and Elmer E. Teare of Cleveland.

He was a lumber dealer of the firm of Potter, Teare & Company and prominently identified with numerous business enterprises. He was a good citizen and much respected.[81]

George Watkins – During the course of our story about the East Cleveland Township Cemetery we learned about George Watkins later in life, now we will explore Mr. Watkins' life and family. Mr. Watkins was born on April 6, 1812 in Chatham, Connecticut. The family departed from East Haddam and arrived in Cleveland in approximately 1818. His father, Timothy, purchased 17 acres of land at the southwest corner of Euclid Avenue and East Madison (now East 79th Street). The area was known as Watkins Glen. Below are George's recollections of life in Cleveland as presented to the Early Settlers Association in 1885.

I was born in the town of Chatham, Middlesex county, Ct., in 1812. My recollections of Cleveland date back to 1818, when my father Timothy Watkins, moved into a log house on Euclid avenue. Five other families came at the same time. Four settled on the west side. These were the families of Josiah Barber, Seth Branch, Martin Kellogg and Thomas O. Young. We came with ox teams, and it took five weeks to make the trip. It was sixty-seven years the 23rd of July, 1885, since we arrived in Cleveland. There were but seventy-five persons all told in Cleveland in 1818.

I was then nearly 7 years old. The appearance of Cleveland at that time is as indelibly fixed upon my mind as though I had seen it yesterday; but when I call to mind the members of each family of pioneers, I find that I am the only one living of that little western-bound caravan and almost the only living representative of this part of the town at that time. Then I realize that a great many years have passed and that my eyes do indeed behold a great city, with scores of churches and schools and great marts of trade, where as a child I only saw rude homes and an almost unbroken forest.

My first recollection of a school-house was of one on Fairmount street, and a second, a block log house on Giddings avenue. This was built in 1822 and I began to attend there the same year. The building was about 15X20 feet. It was called a block house because the logs were hewn on both sides. It was lighted by five windows. The old stone fireplace was six feet across. On three sides of the room was a platform seven or eight feet wide and about one foot high. An upright – board was placed a foot or so from the edge of this platform. Here the little children sat, the board serving for the back of their seats. On the platform and against the walls at the proper height was the writing desk of the older pupils. This desk was continuous around three sides of the room. The seats; like the desk, were of unplanned slabs, which ran parallel with the desk. When it was writing time the boys and girls had to swing their feet over and proceed to business. We wrote with a goose quill, and every morning the master set our copies and mended our pens. Theodore G. Wallace was my first man teacher and Margaret Kidd my first woman teacher.

We had school but three months in the year, in the winter, and it was no small labor to get ready for this comparatively short time. Everybody was poor, there was no money in the country.

Mother spun the yarn and then wove the cloth for our clothes; then it was taken to Newburgh and fulled and colored, and brought home and made up for us. Each year father killed a beast. The skin was taken to the tanner's, and put in the vats, where it lay one year. It was dressed in November, and then our shoes were made. Everybody intended to have the children ready for school about the first Monday in December.

This opening day was a great event in the backwoods of Cleveland in 1822. The organization of the school would seem a little strange now. The teacher was chosen not so much from his knowledge of books as because he had no other business. He was paid the enormous sum of $10 a month and boarded himself. It was often a hard thing to raise even this $10 to pay him.

On the first morning, just at 9 o'clock, the new teacher stepped to the door and shouted, "Boys and girls come into school." We obeyed promptly. The next command was issued, "Now take your seats," which we proceeded to do. Then we were classed. The first class were those in the English Reader, the second in the American Preceptor, the third in the New Testament, the fourth in Webster's spelling-book. We read all around, class by class, before recess; and after, we read again and spelled, standing on the floor. It was a *great honor to be at the head, and keep there three or four days running. We had neither grammar nor geography in any school I ever attended. The arithmetics were Daboll's, Adams' or Pike's, just as the children happened to have. Such a thing as an arithmetic class was unknown. Each scholar who studied that branch worked in his or her seat; when he could not do a sum help was asked from the teacher, who was often puzzled. No one went farther than the rule of three and he was considered a smart boy who could master that.*

This school on Giddings avenue had twenty-five or thirty Scholars. There was no district. Everybody came. The children who came the greatest distance were from a house on what is now the Weddell property. We had school from 9 o'clock in the morning to 4 in the afternoon, six days in the week. In those days the master never spoiled the boys by sparing the rod. Oh, no! He kept four or five rods seasoning amongst the logs and always carried a ruler eighteen inches long in his hand to touch up unruly boys. At Christmas we planned to bar out the teacher, nor did he get in until he furnished a pint of whiskey.

As far as I know, I am the only living representative of this school for the winters of 1822 and '23. This school-house was built later than the other on Fairmount street, which stood on the lot now occupied by the late W. E. Preston. As this did not belong to the district which I have chosen I shall only mention it.

In this school-house on Giddings were held the first religious services that were held in this part of Cleveland. The first preachers were John Crawford, Ira Eddy and Billings O. Plimpton. They are all dead but Billings O. Plimpton, who is now living at an advanced age on the West side. He was the first preacher I ever heard. This was in 1820. He had been a circuit rider from 1817. These three men were on a circuit which reached from Lake Erie to the Ohio river, until the Cuyahoga circuit was formed in 1818. This new circuit took in about all the Western Reserve. The preachers appointed for it were Ezra Booth and Dennis Garland. In that early day all the preachers were Methodists. In 1820 the first Methodist class was formed at Euclid. Dennis Cooper and wife, Ruel House and wife, and three or four others formed the class and met for years in private houses.

The first camp meeting was held at Newburgh by Elder Swazzy in 1802. In 1827 the first class was formed at Doan's corners. The members were Aaron Hubbard and wife, Israel Hubbard (who is still living) and wife, James Sawtell and wife, Ellen Collier, William Mitchell, Samuel Rand, Harriet Slate, Oliver Marshall, Annie Cozad, Philena Gould, Timothy Hurlbut and Nathan Smith. The services were held in private houses until after the stone school-house was built in what is now the old burying ground, after which they were held there.

The first Methodist house of worship at the east end was built about 1840. In the early days we had preaching once in three months, sometimes oftener if it happened that a circuit rider could get over his ground a little earlier. We hailed his coming with de-light.

In 1818 there were only fourteen houses between Fairmount street and Erie. Euclid avenue was called the great road to Erie. Fairmount street was known as the road to Newburgh. Newburgh was at that time of more importance than Cleveland to the early settlers, because it had a gristmill, a sawmill, carding-machine and fulling-mill. Below Erie street a village had been incorporated in 1814. Up to 1825 the entire population east of the Cuyahoga river amounted to but five hundred persons.

From Fairmount street to Erie street, in 1820, there was not a single road leading either north or south from Euclid. This road was very sandy. There were plenty of stumps in it and trees still growing. It was so narrow in places that it was impossible for teams to pass each other. Many of the stumps were not removed till 1840. A man named Cole was riding along one windy night, when a limb from a tree in the road fell upon him, breaking his leg, and he also received other injuries which resulted in his death.

We will commence on the north side of Euclid avenue and mention each house as it stood in 1818, and then go back to our starting-point and take the south side in the same way. We must bear in mind that this time was sixty-seven years ago, more than the ordinary limit of most men's lives, and yet a few have been spared to speak of that period when the ax of the pioneer was busy with clearings which were eventually to be adorned with a fair and prosperous city. The house, nearest Fairmount street, on the north side, was a two-story tavern, owned by Job Doan, and kept by Seth C. Baldwin. The second was a two-story frame, where P. H. Babcock now lives. This was owned by Shadrach Husted, and was burned down in 1822. The third was a log house, where Mrs. Washington lived. This was occupied by James Cole, who owned a small farm there. The fourth house was the one-and a-half story frame of Cardy Parker, where Tilden avenue reaches Euclid. The fifth was the log house of John Bunce, on the corner of Madison and Euclid.

The sixth house was where Harriet Spangler now lives, owned by a man named Tillison, who was the first settler on this Buffalo road. The seventh was a log house, which stood where the east Cleveland car barns now stand. This was owned by William Temple, whose farm was the first of the ten-acre lots into which a part of the city was divided in those early days. The eighth was a one-story frame, which stood on the vacant lot of H. P. Weddell, and was owned by John Norton, a shoemaker. There was no other house to Erie street, but a long stretch of woods.

To go back on the south side, beginning again at Fairmount street, the first house was a one-story frame, which stood back from the road near Doan street. It was owned by Judge H. Strong, who owned at one time nearly all the land at the east end. The second house was a one-story frame, which stood where the Congregational church now stands. This belonged to Ahimaaz Sherman, sr. The third house, a log, stood right at the corner of Lincoln avenue and Euclid. This was owned by Cardy Parker. My father moved there in August, in 1818, and we, lived there one year without either doors or windows. The fourth was a block house, so called because the logs were hewed on both sides. This was the house to which all the people fled when, soon after Perry's victory on the lake, they saw a vessel come into the river from which troops disembarked. They supposed that the British had come to pillage the town. When word came that these were Perry's victorious men returned, the joy of these frightened people even exceeded their fear. This block house was owned by Walter Strong, and was situated near where Mr. Thomas now lives.

The fifth house was a frame on the Bolton place, owned by John Riddle. The sixth was a log house which stood at the corner of Kennard, and was owned by Smith Towner. Nathan Truscott was once tending a coal pit for my father, near Garden street, at night. Thinking that everything was safe, he started home across the swamp about 1 o'clock. On the way wolves attacked him. The dog showed fight and the wolves killed and ate him. This gave Truscott the start, but the wolves were soon on the scent again. He remembered the log house, which was empty at the time, and made for it. The wolves were just behind him. An old ladder happened to be left in the house. With this he was soon out of their reach upon the beams. They were inside and he reached down and closed the door.

When the morning dawned he tore some of the split shingles off the roof and escaped. He got some of the neighbors and they soon killed the wolves. After this house there was no clearing to Erie street.

The Indians had cut down most of the smaller trees for fire-wood on both sides of the road, but the great forest trees and underbrush remained.

If you have noticed, there were only fourteen houses on both sides of this great Buffalo road in 1818. There were no changes until 1820 when several families moved in, amongst whom were Samuel Spangler, Rufus Dunham, John O. Willard, Amos Haloday, Jehial Triscott and Nathan Triscott.

In some later paper I shall hope to give some idea of the manner of life in that early time as I remember it, of the hardships and pleasures of pioneer life, and to show how the sturdy principles of

New England became the cornerstone upon which the honor and integrity of the Western Reserve was founded.[82]

A story is told of one very cold winter day, when Mr. Watkins cut 100 cords of wood in what is now Wade Park, loaded the wood onto his wagon and hauled it downtown. He then piled the wood on Euclid Avenue, east of the old Union Club, and invited any family without wood to help themselves.[83]

S. J. Kelly remembers George Watkins as:

> *Years ago I knew a jovial bearded man named George Watkins, an old resident of the first East Cleveland. Everybody in our neighborhood knew George. Coming along Euclid on the blistering sandy sidewalk on a hot day, or tramping through high snowdrifts, he would call your name before he got to you, shake your hands heartily, inquire about your family and yourself. He was the proprietor of a small grocery west of the Willson Avenue (now East 55th Street) streetcar barns on the north side of Euclid. Yet I remember that he seemed equally well acquainted a'l the way to Doan's Corners.*
>
> *It was said that a Watkins built the first log school house on Sheriff Winslow's place near Giddings Brook that flowed through Watkins Glen. Could the Glen be named after George Watkins? I investigated and the whole story came true.*[84]

Mr. Watkins passed away in 1902 and resides with his family surrounding him in Section 2, Lot 37.

John Welch -

The Late John Welch
  A Brief Sketch of a Well-Known Old Citizen – Offered The Flats For A Horse

> *Mr. John Welch, who died June 11, 1887, at the home of his daughter, Mrs. Randall Crawford, at No. 174 Kennard street, was well-known*

all over the city and county. He was confined to his bed only one day, and though he had been suffering for a short time from a cold, his family had no thought of such a sudden departure. The shock was great to his friends and family, by whom he was greatly beloved. He had lived with his daughter twenty-eight years, and his loss to her will be felt most keenly. Mr. Welch was born on the twenty-sixth of October, 1800, in Duchess county, New York. He went to Courtland county, New York, in 1805, and from there to Cuyahoga county, in 1825. He was married to Mrs. Rebecca Merchant Young, in 1826. Mr. Welch lived on one farm in Euclid township thirty-three years. He was a commissioned officer in the militia several years, and trustee of Euclid township for sixteen years. He was also trustee in East Cleveland township three years, and county commissioner one term. Mr. Welch was engaged in no active business since 1859, but always had a keen interest in all public matters, casting his vote for what he considered right up to the year of his death. He united with the Methodist Church at an early day, and was always a most devoted and earnest worker in the cause of Christianity. He was first and prominent in all good works, considering nothing a hardship when his church was concerned. Mr. Welch came to this part of the country with a horse and fifteen dollars in money. He was offered all of the Flats, from the mouth of the river to where the Standard Oil Works now are, for the horse. The land was nothing but a swamp, and he refused the bargain. He also assisted in laying out Euclid avenue and first improving it. Mr. Welch retained his memory of these early days to the last, and was always happy to meet with old friends and talk about them. He retained the use of his mental faculties to the end, and passed away without a struggle.[85]

Frederick Willson (Brigadier General) – Brigadier General Willson or General Willson as most called him was born on January 4, 1807 in Phelps, Ontario County, New York a descendent of Henry Willson an Irish born immigrant who served in the Revolutionary War. He arrived in Cuyahoga County in 1830 and settled in Mayfield Township. Government land was purchased where Mr. Willson built a gristmill. The area around the mill which was located near the Chagrin River became known as Willson's Mills/Wilson's Mill. The first post office for the area was situated at Willson's Mills. In 1839 the mill burned to the ground but was immediately rebuilt and back in operation by January 7,

1840. Willson's Mills ceased to exist sometime after 1894. Wilson Mills Road still exists today and was named after General Willson.

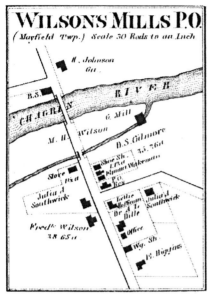

Willson's Mills Business Directory.

R. Worts, Jr., Manufacturer of and Dealer in Carriages, Buggies, Sleighs, Cutters, and light and heavy Wagons, at Mayfield Centre.

Geo. A. Bennett, General Blacksmith, at Mayfield Centre.

Geo. Hill, Justice of the Peace, Lot 20.

Chas. L. Sherman, Manufacturer of all kinds of Lumber, Siding, Flooring, Shingles, Lath, and Handles of every description.

M. H. Willson, Proprietor of Gristmill.

Albert Granger, Justice of the Peace, Lot 46.

D. S. Gilmore, Proprietor of Sawmill.

1874 Atlas of Cuyahoga County, Titus, Simmons & Titus

General Willson married Eliza (nee Henderson) on September 6, 1836. Mrs. Willson was born on November 25, 1816 in Columbia County, New York the daughter of Ira and Elizabeth (nee Hopp) Henderson. There were nine children born of the marriage.

General Willson began his military service with a regiment of the light artillery in the New York Militia. In 1834 he was elected Major of the Second Brigade, Ninth Division, Ohio Militia. He continued to be promoted until in 1838 he was promoted to the rank of Brigadier General. In approximately 1842 he retired from military service. General Willson served as Justice of the Peace for six year and was a member for 60 years in the Masonic fraternity reaching the rank of Sir Knight.

General Willson passed away on July 21, 1884 at the age of 78. He and his wife, Eliza and a number of their children rest in Section 6, Lot 52.

John S. Wisner (original subscriber of the Publick Burying Ground) was located living in Cleveland with his wife, two sons and three daughters in the 1830 census. In the 1840 census he is found living with his family in Rutland, Lake County, Ohio. After this date he and his family could not be located.

Daniel Parnell Yea – Born in Newton Abbott District, County of Devon, England in 1851, he married his wife Margaret Howe in March, 1872 in the same location. According to the census records he was carpenter by trade and arrived in the United States in 1876. Very little information is available on the Yea family, yet the monument that stands tall in Section 9, Lot 74 calls out for attention. Family members could not explain the basis for the design on the monument. However, it was not uncommon for anchors to be utilized in Christian settings to disguise a cross. It was meant to keep us from drifting off course thereby firmly anchoring us to beliefs. The ivy interwoven in the anchor represents immortality. The other reason for the anchor could be to represent a sailor.

Author Photograph Collection

Table 1: Allocation of Shares

Name	Shares	Name	Shares
Ahimaaz Sherwin, Sen.	2	Andrew Cozad	1
Timothy Watkins	2	William Hudson	1
Aaron Hubbard	2	Benj. Clark	1
Job Doan	2	Humphrey Nichols	1
James Strong	2	Casper Noel	1
John Shenefelt	2	Jesse Nichols	1
Ezra Graves	2	Nathan Ingersoll	1
Richard H. Blinn	2	John Sherman	1
Elijah Ingersoll	1	John Gould	1
Sam. Spangler	1	Ahimaaz Sherwin, Jun.	1
Daniel Pangborn	1	Andrew Logan	1
Amos Kingsbury	1	Sam Dibble	1
Nathaniel Marshall	1	Seth Baldwin	1
Joseph Butler	1	Elias Cozad	1
Harvey Sumner	1	William Kirk	1
John Wisner	1	Two additional names are unreadable.	

Table 2: Lot Assignments in the Publick Burying Ground

Name	Lot	Name	Lot
John Shenefelt	18	Aaron Hubbard	35
Sam Dibble	30	William Kirk	4
John Sherman	32	Ahimaaz Sherwin, Sr.	22
Job Doan	1	Richard H. Blinn	6
Humphrey Nichols	15	Timothy Watkins	23
Ezra Graves	9	Elijah Ingersoll	36
Seth C. Baldwin	2	Andrew Logan	12
Sam. Spangler	24	Andrew Cozad	10
Nathaniel Marshall	8	Timothy Watkins	42
Joseph Butler	33	Amos Kingsbury	40
Ahimaaz Sherwin, Sr.	28	Harvey Sumner	21
Ahimaaz Sherwin, Jr.	27	Daniel Pangborn	20
John S. Wisner	5	Benj. Clark	19
Nathan Ingersoll	31	Ezra Graves	38
Elias Cozad	11	James Strong	41
John Shenefelt	13	Aaron Hubbard	29
John Gould	39	Job Doan	37
James Strong	3	Casper Noel	26
William Hudson	16	Richard H. Blinn	25
Jesse Nichols	34		

Table 3: Compilation of George Watkins, et al and Euclid Avenue Congregational Church Records

Lot(s)	Name	Amount	Part of Burying Ground	Relationships/Notes	Lot Ownership Transferred To	Deed Recorded
	Aumick, John	40.00	West	Deed indicates amount paid was $5.00	John W. Heisley	
	Barber, Timothy (Samantha)	25.00	East	No lot in her name - 1 Body		
	Barber, Mr. & Mrs. Jefferson	5.00			John W. Heisley	
	Billings, Charles W. & Susan	10.00	West	Living in Oconomowic, Wackesha County, WI	George Watkins	
	Billings, Seth M.	10.00	West	He was living in WI.	George Watkins	
	Billings, Sylvester	10.00	West		George Watkins	
	Bishop, C.D.	8.00				
	Burton, Abby	5.00	West	Deed indicates amount paid was $1.00	John W. Heisley	
	Burton, E.D.	15.00	West	Son of Dr. Burton	George Watkins	Vol. 438, Page 49
	Chadwick, Mr. & Mrs. George	5.00	West		John W. Heisley	
	Cody, J.A.	20.00	West			
	Cole, Daniel W.	25.00	East	No lot in his name – 2 Bodies. Deed indicates amount paid was $1.00	John W. Heisley	
	Connor, Emma R.	5.00			John W. Heisley	
	Coon, Mary A. (Kuhn)	25.00	West	Deed indicates amount paid was $5.00	John W. Heisley	
10	Cozad, Andrew				Euclid Avenue Congregational Church	
	Cozad, Samuel				Euclid Avenue Congregational Church	

149

Lot(s)	Name	Part of Burying Ground	Amount	Relationships/Notes	Lot Ownership Transferred To	Deed Recorded
22	Crawford, Clay	West	25.00	Heir of B. Crawford	John W. Heisley	Vol. 421, Page 442
22	Crawford, Francis	West	25.00	Heir of B. Crawford	John W. Heisley	Vol. 421, Page 446
	Crawford, Lynda	West	20.00			
	Crook, Emaline & S.A.		10.00	Deed indicates $1.00 was paid and was dated 3/31/1875.	John W. Heisley	
31	Crosby, T.D.	East	25.00	Heir of N. Ingersoll - Lot 31	John W. Heisley	Vol. 421, Page 444
	Dean, Phebe Ann		20.00		George Watkins	Vol. 421, Page 449
	Decker, B. S. (Duke) & Sophia M.	West	30.00	Deed indicates amount paid was $1.00	John W. Heisley	Vol. 421, Page 437
	Dille, J.S. & Elenor	East	20.00	Wife of J.S. - Lot 18 - In Name of Shenefelt. Deed indicates amount paid was $5.00	John W. Heisley	
1 and 37	Doan			Heir of Dr. Burton. Deed indicates lot was purchased by John W. Heisley	George Watkins	
	Dodge, Lucy A.	West	1.00		George Watkins	Vol. 436, Page 318
22	Dunham, Alfred A.	West	22.00	Heir of B. Crawford	John W. Heisley	Vol. 421, Page 441
	Duty, Elizabeth	West	20.00			
	Eddy, Samuel		30.00	Deed indicates $25.00 was paid and was dated 2/20/1877.	George Watkins	

Lot(s)	Name	Amount	Part of Burying Ground	Relationships/Notes	Lot Ownership Transferred To	Deed Recorded
	Edwards, Hannah	5.00			John W. Heisley	
	Fenton, Sarah D.	21.00	East	Daughter of T. H. Watkins, son of T. Watkins.	John W. Heisley	Vo. 421, Page 440
17	Fuller, E.			Heirs of	Euclid Avenue Congregational Church	
	Fuller, E.	5.00			John W. Heisley	
	Gould, Rodney	25.00	West			
31	Hall, Samantha	25.00	East	Heir of N. Ingersoll - Lot 31	John W. Heisley	Vol. 421, Page 443
	Hamilton, DeWitt		West			Vol. 438, Page 50
	Heller, Edwin	10.00	East	Deed to Church	John W. Heisley	
	Hendershot, George B.	25.00	West	Deed indicates amount paid was $5.00	John W. Heisley	
	Hendershot, O.H.P.	12.50	West	Deed indicates amount paid was $5.00	John W. Heisley	
	Hodges, Thomas	16.00	West	3 Lots		
	Hodges, Thomas	60.00	West			
	Hosley, Adolphus	17.00	West			
29 and 35	Hubbard, Israel	10.00	East	Son of Aaron Hubbard	George Watkins	Vol. 436, Page 319
16	Hudson, William P.		East	Heir of Wm. Hudson	John W. Heisley	Vol. 421, Page 449
31	Ingersoll, Barlow	25.00	East	Heir of N. Ingersoll	John W. Heisley	Vol. 421, Page 444
31	Ingersoll, E.B. and Kate	50.00	East	Heir of N. Ingersoll	John W. Heisley	Vol. 421, Page 445

Lot(s)	Name	Amount	Part of Burying Ground	Relationships/Notes	Lot Ownership Transferred To	Deed Recorded
31	Ingersoll, John and Hannah	50.00	East	Heir of N. Ingersoll	George Watkins/J.R. Walters	Vol. 421, Page 447
31	Ingersoll, Laban	26.00	East	No lot in his name.	John W. Heisley	Vol. 421, Page 437
31	Ingersoll, Polly	15.00	East	Heir of N. Ingersoll	John W. Heisley	Vol. 421, Page 444
	Janes, Henry (James, Harry)	10.00	West	Deed indicates amount paid was $1.00	John W. Heisley	
	Johnson, Roland Heirs	25.00	West	Deed is dated 11/6/1876.	George Watkins/J.R. Walters	
31	Kelley, John, heirs	25.00	East	Heir of N. Ingersoll		
31	Kelley, Nathan I. & P	25.00	East	Heirs of N. Ingersoll	George Watkins	Vol. 421, Page 448
	King, Laura	10.00	West	Deed indicates amount paid was $1.00	John W. Heisley	
	King, Poladere	10.00	West	Deed indicates amount paid was $1.00	John W. Heisley	
	Lee, Laura	1.00	West		John W. Heisley	
	McIlrath, M.S.	25.62	West		John W. Heisley	Vol. 421, Page 437
	McIlrath, Sally (Sarah)	1.00	West		John W. Heisley	
	Merchant, Mary Ann	10.00	West	Deed indicates amount paid was $5.00	John W. Heisley	
	Mix		West		George Watkins George Watkins/J. W. Heisley	Vol. 422, Page 16
13	O'Connor, Ransom	12.00				

Lot(s)	Name	Amount	Part of Burying Ground	Relationships/Notes	Lot Ownership Transferred To	Deed Recorded
	Peck, T.D.	10.00	West			
	Plaisted, Ivory & Louisa	16.00	West	Deed indicates $5 was paid and was dated 5/23/1888.	George Watkins	
	Quinlan, Alice F.	5.00			John W. Heisley	
	Rathburn, Nancy	10.00	West			
	Rush, Stephen	25.00	West		George Watkins/J.R. Walters	Vol. 421, Page 449
	Sawtell, Eda	1.00	West		John W. Heisley	
	Saxton, J. C.	25.00	West	Deed indicates amount paid was $5.00	John W. Heisley	
13 and 18	Shenefelt, John	28.00			George Watkins	
	Sherman, Addie M.	5.00			John W. Heisley	
	Sherman, Emeline M.	30.00	West	Deed indicates amount paid was $5.00	John W. Heisley	
	Sherman, J.S.(?)	5.00			John W. Heisley	
	Sherman, Sabina	15.00	West	Deed indicates amount paid was $5.00	John W. Heisley	
27	Sherwin, Ahimaaz	30.00	West	Several Lots	John W. Heisley	
28	Sherwin, Ahimaaz		East	One Lot	John W. Heisley	Vol. 421, Page 439
27 and 28	Sherwin, Sarah	5.00	Same as above			
	Slaght, Joseph	62.62	West	Deed is dated 10/10/1874.	George Watkins	
	Smith, Mercy	1.00	West		John W. Heisley	
	Smith, Richard C.	1.00	West		John W. Heisley	
	Smith, Roseta (Roster)	5.00	West			
	Stark, L.D.	20.00	West	One of Dibble's lots.		

Lot(s)	Name	Amount	Part of Burying Ground	Relationships/Notes	Lot Ownership Transferred To	Deed Recorded
45	Streator, Dr.				Euclid Avenue Congregational Church	
	Thomas, Levi	1.00	West		John W. Heisley	
	Tucker, Maria	12.50		Deed indicates amount paid was $5.00	John W. Heisley	
	Upson, Mary		West		George Watkins	Vol. 436, Page 319
	Warner, Mary P. (Warren)	15.00	West		John W. Heisley	Vol. 421, Page 444
4	Watkins, Hosmer		West	Son of Timothy H. Watkins	George Watkins	Vol. 443, Page 492
	Watson, J.N.		West		George Watkins	Vol. 421, Page 451
22	Wheeler, Eleanor J.	25.00	West	Heir of B. Crawford	John W. Heisley	Vol. 421, Page 441
31	Wood, E.B.		West	Heir of N. Ingersoll	John W. Heisley	Vol. 421, Page 446
	Wyngard		West	Heir of Levi Ingersoll	George Watkins	Vol. 422, Page 15

For Four Lots	60.00
Brickman Handling Stone	2.00
Expenses to Youngstown	3.90
Removing 3 Bodies for Doane	6.00
Making 3 Boxes	3.00
Removing 62 Bodies	
My Services	
Interest on Monies Paid Out	
Cost for G.W. Watkins	50.00

Lots Never Sold
14, 24, 30 and 46

There appear to have been 48 lots in the east half and 70 lots in the west half

Table 4: Transfers from the Publick Burying Ground

Section	Lot	Lot Owner	Transferred To	Section	Lot
	36	Baldwin, Hiram (Purchased from Richard Killbury 10/25/1838)	Niles, Ohio		
East	2	Baldwin, Seth	East Cleveland Township Cemetery	12	21
	43	Bidwell, Joseph (Purchased from Job Doan on 5/20/1832)	Unable to Locate		
West	6	Billings, Levi	Unable to Locate		
West	15	Billings, Levi	Unable to Locate		
West	31	Billings, Levi	Unable to Locate		
West	37	Billings, Levi	Unable to Locate		
West	42	Billings, Levi	Unable to Locate		
East	43	Billings, Levi	Unable to Locate		
East	6	Blinn, R. H.	Unable to Locate		
East	25	Blinn, R. H.	Unable to Locate		
West	8	Burton, Elijah	East Cleveland Township Cemetery	3	43
East	25	Burton, R.	Unable to Locate		
East	23	Case, Hernon	Unable to Locate		
East	19	Clark, Benjamin	Unable to Locate		
West	64	Cody, Issac	East Cleveland Township Cemetery	10	157
West	33	Cole, D. W.	East Cleveland Township Cemetery	3	19
East	44	Compton, S.	East Cleveland Township Cemetery	6	38
West	34	Coon, Mary A. (Purchased from H. Nichols)	East Cleveland Township Cemetery	4	30
East	10	Cozad, Andrew	Lake View Cemetery	6	66
East	11	Cozad, Elias	East Cleveland Township Cemetery	6	1
West	1	Crawford, B.	East Cleveland Township Cemetery	3	8
West	24	Crawford, B.	East Cleveland Township Cemetery	3	8

Section	Lot	Lot Owner	Transferred To	Section	Lot
East	30	Dibble, Sam	Unable to Locate		
East	18	Dille, Jacob (Purchased from John Shenefelt on 1/16/1826)	East Cleveland Township Cemetery	8	23
West	5	Doan, J.	East Cleveland Township Cemetery	6	10, 11, 25 and 26
West	9	Doan, J.	East Cleveland Township Cemetery	6	10, 11, 25 and 26
West	12	Doan, J.	East Cleveland Township Cemetery	6	10, 11, 25 and 26
West	25	Doan, J.	East Cleveland Township Cemetery	6	10, 11, 25 and 26
West	32	Doan, J.	East Cleveland Township Cemetery	6	10, 11, 25 and 26
West	39	Doan, J.	East Cleveland Township Cemetery	6	10, 11, 25 and 26
West	44	Doan, J.	East Cleveland Township Cemetery	6	10, 11, 25 and 26
West	47	Doan, J.	East Cleveland Township Cemetery	6	10, 11, 25 and 26
West	50	Doan, J.	East Cleveland Township Cemetery	2	7,8 and 10
East	1	Doan, Job	Lake View Cemetery		
East	9	Embury, Anthony	Unable to Locate		
East	17	Fuller, Edwin	East Cleveland Township Cemetery	8	2
West	24	Gale, Martin	East Cleveland Township Cemetery	7	10
East	47	Gay, E.	Unable to Locate		
West	10	Gould, John	East Cleveland Township Cemetery	6	36

Section	Lot	Lot Owner	Transferred To	Section	Lot
East	39	Gould, John	East Cleveland Township Cemetery	6	36
East	14	Graves, Ezra	Unable to Locate		
East	38	Graves, Ezra	Unable to Locate		
West	7	Greves, A. (Purchased from H. Nichols)	Unable to Locate		
West	19	Hendershot, Casper (Purchased from E. Burton)	East Cleveland Township Cemetery	7	41
West	40	Hendershot, G.	East Cleveland Township Cemetery	1	9
West	40	Hendershot, G.	East Cleveland Township Cemetery	7	41
East	29	Hubbard, Aaron	Woodland Cemetery	5	8
East	35	Hubbard, Aaron	Woodland Cemetery	5	8
East	16	Hudson, William	East Cleveland Township Cemetery	9	1
West	17	Ingersoll, Elijah	East Cleveland Township Cemetery	5	5
West	20	Ingersoll, Elijah	East Cleveland Township Cemetery	5	5
West	22	Ingersoll, Elijah	East Cleveland Township Cemetery	5	5
East	36	Ingersoll, Elijah	East Cleveland Township Cemetery	5	5
West	38	Ingersoll, Elijah	East Cleveland Township Cemetery	5	5
West	27	Ingersoll, Nathan	East Cleveland Township Cemetery	1	19 and 20
West	28	Ingersoll, Nathan	East Cleveland Township Cemetery	1	19 and 20
East	31	Ingersoll, Nathan	East Cleveland Township Cemetery	1	19 and 20
West	58	Janes, A. (Purchased from O. Janes)	Woodland Cemetery	17	13
West	29	Johnson, Roland	Unable to Locate		
East	37	Kaiser, P.H. (Purchased from Job Doan)	Unable to Locate		
West	11	Kilbury, R.	Unable to Locate		
West	48	Kilbury, R.	Unable to Locate		
West	16	King, J.	Unable to Locate		
West	33	King, J.	Unable to Locate		
West	51	King, J.	Unable to Locate		
East	40	Kingsbury, Amos	Unable to Locate		
East	4	Kirk, William	Unable to Locate		

Section	Lot	Lot Owner	Transferred To	Section	Lot
West	45	Lee, Rowland (Purchased from A. Sherwin 3/15/1833)	East Cleveland Township Cemetery	1	16
West	42	Little, D.	Unable to Locate		
East	12	Logan, Andrew	Moved out of State		
West	23	McIlrath, Michael	East Cleveland Township Cemetery	1	7
West	35	McIlrath, Michael	East Cleveland Township Cemetery	1	7
West	43	Myers, (Mr.)	Unable to Locate		
West	14	Name Unreadable			
East	15	Nichols, Humphrey	Woodland Cemetery	31	18
West	52	Nichols, Humphrey	Woodland Cemetery	31	18
East	34	Nichols, Jesse	Woodland Cemetery	31	18
East	26	Noel, Casper	Unable to Locate		
West	56	None Identified	Unable to Locate		
West	57	None Identified	Unable to Locate		
West	59	None Identified	Unable to Locate		
West	61	None Identified	Unable to Locate		
West	62	None Identified	Unable to Locate		
West	63	None Identified	Unable to Locate		
West	66	None Identified	Unable to Locate		
West	67	None Identified	Unable to Locate		
West	70	None Identified	Unable to Locate		
West	13	O'Connor, Damon	East Cleveland Township Cemetery	1	24, 25, 26, 27 and 28
West	55	Ormiston, A.	East Cleveland Township Cemetery	3	2
East	20	Pangborn, Daniel	Unable to Locate		
East	26	Patterson, Grunsfried J.	Unable to Locate		
West	60	Peck, P. W.	East Cleveland Township Cemetery	7	21 and 22
East	33	Rhodes, Lyman (Purchased from Joseph Butler)	East Cleveland Township Cemetery	5	51
East	13	Shenefelt, John	Unable to Locate		
East	32	Sherman, John	East Cleveland Township Cemetery	9	18 and 19
West	37	Sherman, John	East Cleveland Township Cemetery	9	18 and 19
West	26	Sherwin, Ahimaaz	Lake View Cemetery	1	

Section	Lot	Lot Owner	Transferred To	Section	Lot
East	28	Sherwin, Ahimaaz	Lake View Cemetery	1	
West	49	Sherwin, Ahimaaz	Lake View Cemetery	1	
East	22	Sherwin, Ahimaaz (Sr.)	East Cleveland Township Cemetery	8	29, 30, 31 and 32
East	27	Sherwin, Ahimaaz (Sr.)	East Cleveland Township Cemetery	8	29, 30, 31 and 32
West	36	Slaght, Joseph	East Cleveland Township Cemetery	3	20 and 21
West	46	Slaght, Joseph	East Cleveland Township Cemetery	3	20 and 21
East	25	Slate, G. H.	Unable to Locate		
West	69	Smith, R.G.	Unable to Locate		
East	24	Spangler, Sam P.	East Cleveland Township Cemetery	8	14
West	45	Streeter, W.	Unable to Locate		
East	3	Strong, James	East Cleveland Township Cemetery	1	21
East	41	Strong, James	East Cleveland Township Cemetery	1	21
East	21	Sumner, Harvey (Henry)	Unable to Locate		
West	30	Thomas, P.	Unable to Locate		
East	46	Walters, S.	East Cleveland Township Cemetery	3	19
West	2	Watkins, George	East Cleveland Township Cemetery	2	37
West	3	Watkins, George	East Cleveland Township Cemetery	2	37
West	4	Watkins, George	East Cleveland Township Cemetery	2	37
West	18	Watkins, George (Transfer to W. Watkins)	East Cleveland Township Cemetery	2	37
East	42	Watkins, Timothy	East Cleveland Township Cemetery	2	37
East	8	Watkins, Timothy (Purchased from Nathaniel Marshall)	East Cleveland Township Cemetery	2	37
West	21	Watkins, Timothy from John (Surname unreadable)	East Cleveland Township Cemetery	2	37
West	25	Watts, S.R.	Unable to Locate		
West	65	White, Samuel	Unable to Locate		
West	55	Widdell, M.	Unable to Locate		
West	68	Wisner, H.	Unable to Locate		
East	5	Wisner, John T.	Unable to Locate		
West	40	Wood, H.	Unable to Locate		
East	7	Young, A.	East Cleveland Township Cemetery	3	40

Table 5: Transfers to East Cleveland Township Cemetery from the Publick Burying Ground

Last Name	First Name	Middle Name	Section	Lot	Date of Interment	Date of Death	Transfered From
Albee	Mary		11	8	10/29/1860	9/19/1838	Doan's Corner
Baldwin	Seth	Cogswell	12	21		9/22/1828	Doan's Corner
Beckwith	Elvira		8	3	5/1/1860	4/8/1859	Doan's Corner
Bennett	Ida	May	3	11	5/6/1862		Doan's Corner
Burton	Elijah		3	43	11/21/1859	4/2/1854	Doan's Corner
Burton	Mary		3	43	11/21/1859	9/3/1827	Doan's Corner
Cody	Hannah	M.	8	32	12/6/1860		Doan's Corner
Cozad	Anna		2	20	5/2/1862	9/14/1828	Doan's Corner
Cozad	Minerva		2	20	5/2/1862		Doan's Corner
Cozad	N.	Clark	2	20	5/2/1862	9/23/1828	Doan's Corner
Dille	Carey		8	23	5/9/1860	1/1/1857	Doan's Corner
Dille	Jeanette		8	23	5/9/1860	7/6/1857	Doan's Corner
Doan	Timothy		2	7		2/4/1847	Doan's Corner
Doane	Eliza		2	7	3/12/1861	3/9/1851	Doan's Corner
Doane	Jared	P.	2	7		5/9/1853	Doan's Corner
Doane	Lewis		2	8		1/19/1858	Doan's Corner
Doane	Polly		2	7		8/12/1839	Doan's Corner
Doane	Timothy		2	7		5/30/1842	Doan's Corner
Doane	Timothy		6	10		4/3/1828	Doan's Corner

160

Last Name	First Name	Middle Name	Section	Lot	Date of Interment	Date of Death	Transferred From
Dorsh	Layfatte	L.	8	14	5/16/1860		Doan's Corner
Dorsh	Samuel	M.	8	14	5/16/1860		Doan's Corner
Edwards	Adonijah		12	5		1/9/1831	Doan's Corner
Edwards	Anna		12	3		6/19/1833	Doan's Corner
Edwards	Polly		12	3		2/18/1832	Doan's Corner
Edwards	Rhoda	Fay	12	3		3/29/1859	Doan's Corner
Edwards	Rodolphus		12	5		7/17/1840	Doan's Corner
Fortes	Sabra	Ann	8	30	4/11/1862		Doan's Corner
Francisco	Sarah		8	4	5/1/1860	1/1/1858	Doan's Corner
Gardner	Achsa		8	30	4/11/1862		Doan's Corner
Gardner	C. M.	Clay	8	3	4/11/1862		Doan's Corner
Hendershot	Casper		7	41	4/8/1861	8/19/1842	Doan's Corner
Hendershot	George		7	41	4/8/1861		Doan's Corner
Hendershot	Sarah	M	8	19	4/13/1861		Doan's Corner
Hudson	Barclay		2	3	8/28/1862	10/10/1852	Doan's Corner
Hudson	Colon	Fordyce	9	1	12/18/1861	7/1/1823	Doan's Corner
Hudson	Horace	A.	9	1	12/18/1861	3/2/1829	Doan's Corner
Hudson	John	C.	9	17	8/28/1862	8/19/1857	Doan's Corner
Johnson	Isaac		9	25	11/30/1862		Doan's Corner
King	George	W.	8	5	4/25/1861	8/13/1857	Doan's Corner
Kreager	Margaret	J. Welch	3	39	4/30/1860	2/19/1856	Doan's Corner
O'Connor	Lawrence		1	24		7/22/1840	Doan's Corner

Last Name	First Name	Middle Name	Section	Lot	Date of Interment	Date of Death	Transfered From
O'Connor	Phoebe		1	24		8/11/1854	Doan's Corner
O'Connor	Ransom		1	24		1/1/1835	Doan's Corner
Olmstead	Anna		12	3		11/17/1830	Doan's Corner
Peck	Baby		7	22	2/7/1860		Doan's Corner
Peck	Frances	C.	7	21	2/7/1860		Doan's Corner
Peck	Geraldo	A.	7	21	2/7/1860	2/2/1852	Doan's Corner
Post	Frances		1	23	1/27/1860	1/1/1852	Doan's Corner
Post	Helen	E.	1	23	1/27/1860	1/1/1853	Doan's Corner
Rhodes	Lyman		12	3			Doan's Corner
Ruple	Mary	Alice	8	5	4/25/1861	6/20/1863	Doan's Corner
Salter	William		11	7	10/22/1860	11/17/1856	Doan's Corner
Secbos	Julia	Post	1	22	4/11/1861		Doan's Corner
Sherwin	Ahimaaz		8	32	12/6/1860	12/31/1839	Doan's Corner
Sherwin	Hannah		8	32	12/6/1860	6/26/1828	Doan's Corner
Sherwin	Ruth	Day	8	32	12/6/1860	5/19/1833	Doan's Corner
Slaght	Adelaide	T.	3	20	4/24/1860		Doan's Corner
Slaght	Darwin	E.	2	19	4/24/1860		Doan's Corner
Slaght	Taphenis		3	21	4/24/1860	10/4/1851	Doan's Corner

Last Name	First Name	Middle Name	Section	Lot	Date of Interment	Date of Death	Transferred From
Smith	Anna	Mariah	8	21	2/27/1860		Doan's Corner
Smith	Emma	Gertrude	8	21	2/27/1860		Doan's Corner
Smith	Richard	Myers	8	21	2/27/1860		Doan's Corner
Spangler	Eliza		8	14	5/16/1860	1/1/1834	Doan's Corner
Towner	Amanda	M.	7	17	9/7/1861		Doan's Corner
Towner	D.	D.	7	17	9/7/1861		Doan's Corner
Towner	Leverett	S.	7	17	9/7/1861	3/24/1843	Doan's Corner
Towner	Merritt		7	17	9/7/1861		Doan's Corner
Towner	S.	A.	7	17	9/7/1861		Doan's Corner
Towner	Smith		7	17	9/7/1861	8/11/1833	Doan's Corner
Wallace	Charlotte		10	7	5/2/1862		Doan's Corner
Walther	Margaret		11	9	10/27/1860	1/1/1857	Doan's Corner
Welch	George	W.	3	41	4/30/1860	7/19/1829	Doan's Corner
Welch	Lillian	J.	3	41	4/30/1860		Doan's Corner
Welch	Rebecca		3	40	4/30/1860	1/21/1849	Doan's Corner
Weston	Nancy	Elvira	7	41	4/8/1861		Doan's Corner
Young	Robert		3	40	4/30/1860	7/18/1825	Doan's Corner

Table 6: Transfers to East Cleveland Township Cemetery from "Private Ground", et al

Last Name	First Name	Middle Name	Section	Lot	Date of Interment	Date of Death	Transferred From
Adams	Harriet	S.	2	29	12/7/1859		Collamer
Adams	Sarah	M.	2	28	12/7/1859	3/18/1820	Collamer
Adams	William		2	28	12/7/1859	12/20/1840	Collamer
Bennett	Sevantia	Dille	1	4	6/28/1862		Euclid
							Private
Boot	Sophronia	Jones	2	16	4/26/1860	3/12/1854	Ground
							Private
Brainard	Julia	S.	2	14	4/26/1860	8/1/1853	Ground
Cahoon	Polly		10	8	9/26/1862	10/12/1841	Collamer
Cahoon	Reynolds		10	8	9/22/1862	4/5/1844	Collamer
Camp	Byron		1	17	6/28/1862		Euclid
Camp	Sophia	W.	1	17	6/28/1862		Euclid
Camp	William	M.	1	17	6/28/1862		Euclid
Coit	Mary	Breed	6	17	3/3/1860	3/18/1856	Euclid
							Private
Cozad	Cynthia	L.	6	1	4/30/1860	7/16/1845	Ground

164

Last Name	First Name	Middle Name	Section	Lot	Date of Interment	Date of Death	Transferred From
Cozad	Ethan	A.B.	6	1	4/30/1860	12/29/1849	Private Ground
Cozad	H.	Amelia	6	1	4/30/1860	9/5/1847	Private Ground
Dille	Candace		1	4	6/28/1862		Euclid
Dille	Elizabeth		1	4	6/28/1862		Euclid
Dille	G. or J.	W.	1	4	6/28/1862		Euclid
Dille	Harrison		1	4	6/28/1862		Euclid
Dille	S.	Milliard	1	4	6/28/1862		Euclid
Ford	Darius		2	42	3/27/1860		Private Ground
Ford	Eunice	Orcutt	2	42	3/27/1860		Private Ground
Ford	Hezekiah		2	41	3/27/1860	12/19/1848	Private Ground
Ford	Lewis		2	18	3/16/1860	6/7/1854	Private Ground
Ford	Louretta				7/7/1893		Lake View Cemetery

Last Name	First Name	Middle Name	Section	Lot	Date of Interment	Date of Death	Transferred From
Garrett	Carrie		13	41	10/22/1895		Lake View Cemetery
Harris	Margot		14				Private Grounds
Hubbell	Harriet	A.	4	42	9/12/1939		Lake View Cemetery
Hutchinson	A.	G.	3	5	12/12/1861		Collamer
Jones	Benjamin		2	1	4/26/1860	11/20/1854	Private Ground
Jones	Edmond	B.	2	15	4/26/1860	2/28/1856	Private Ground
Jones	Eliza	Brainard	2	16	4/26/1860	4/28/1858	Private Ground
Jones	Harriett	E.	2	16	4/26/1860	5/15/1851	Private Ground
Jones	Lydia	A.	2	16	4/26/1860	9/13/1851	Private Ground
Jones	Nancy	M.	2	15	4/26/1860	6/4/1852	Private Ground
Logan	Caroline	M.	8	30	10/29/1896		Lake View Cemetery

Last Name	First Name	Middle Name	Section	Lot	Date of Interment	Date of Death	Transfered From
Norton	Samuel	G.	7	8	4/30/1861	11/16/1848	Twinsburgh
Smith	Amy		7	35	3/3/1860		Collamer
Smith	G. or S.		1	4	6/28/1862		Euclid
Stampfli	Fred		10	265	1/28/1903		Woodland Cemetery
Stephens	Thomas		10	1	11/6/1862		St. Clair Road
Tyler	Almerin	D.	8	36	4/21/1862	1/1/1855	Farm
Tyler	Daniel	S.	8	36	4/14/1862	6/8/1843	Farm
Walker	Courtney	Ann	12	51	7/19/1894		Woodland Cemetery
Warner	George		8	4	8/6/1888	8/4/1888	Woodland Cemetery
Watkins	Adalie		2	37		1/1/1843	Private Ground
Watkins	Anna	Eliza	2	37		1/1/1841	Private Ground
Watkins	Russell		2	37		1/1/1841	Private Ground

Last Name	First Name	Middle Name	Section	Lot	Date of Interment	Date of Death	Transferred From
Watkins	Sophia		2	37		1/1/1846	Private Ground
Watkins	Timothy		2	37		9/2/1830	Private Ground
Watkins	Timothy		2	37		1/1/1843	Private Ground
Watkins	Watson		2	37		1/1/1855	Private Ground
West	Alice	Harmon	6	16	12/15/1859	12/25/1853	Euclid
West	Clara	Elizabeth	6	16	12/15/1859	7/6/1852	Euclid
West	Elizabeth		6	16	12/15/1859	4/13/1850	Euclid
West	Harriet	E.	6	18	12/7/1859	9/12/1856	Euclid
West	John		6	16	12/15/1859	6/10/1842	Euclid
White	Mary	E.	13	28	10/13/1898		Woodland Cemetery

Table 7: Military Veterans

Last Name	First Name	Middle Name	War	Section	Lot	Grave	Row
Albright	George	W.	Civil War	10	100	J	
Aldridge	Richard	A.	World War1	11	20	M	
Allison	Robert	F.	Civil War	11	South Plot	143	7
Alvord	Daniel	M.	Civil War	10	41	D	
Ambrose	Charles		Spanish American War	11	South Plot	208	14
Ambrose	Cornelius		Regular Service	10	36	H	
Anderson	Barney		War of 1812	6	31	B	
Anderson	Charles	alias Smith	Spanish American War	11	South Plot	209	14
Ault	Theodore	J.	World War1	13	29	J	
Badger	David	P.	Civil War	11	80	G	
Baker	Henry	B.	Civil War	11	North Plot	100	14
Baldwin	Seth	Cogswell	Revolutionary War	12	21	A	
Ball	Andrew	J.	Civil War	11	23 or 28	Single Grave	
Bardwell	William	E.	Civil War	10	69	I	
Barnes	Eli	Augustus	Civil War	6	37	J	
Barnes	Frederick	E.	Spanish American War	6	37	B	
Barney	Luke		War of 1812	1	1	B	
Barnhard	William		World War1	7	25	J	
Barnum	John	N.	Civil War	11	63	G	
Bartlett	John	P.	Civil War	10	3	F	
Bastian	Edward		Undetermined	1	76	C	
Bastin	William		Spanish American War	11		182	
Beam	Gale	R.	World War1	7	58	A	
Beard	George		Civil War	11	South Plot	230	16
Beeman	Norman		Civil War	2	85	B	
Beers	John	P.	Civil War	3	31	A	
Bergin	John	(Bergan)	Civil War	10	38	I	
Berry	Harry		World War1	10	30	E	
Birth	Otto	C.	World War1	5	94	C	

Last Name	First Name	Middle Name	War	Section	Lot	Grave	Row
Black	Aretus	E.	Civil War	10	86	A	
Blackburn	William	P.	World War1	10	East Plot	438	37
Backstock	Samuel	H.	World War1	10	147	B	
Blaschke	Herman	R.	Indian War	12	41		
Blue	Alfred		Civil War	6	61		
Boehringer	Peter	J.	Civil War	10	East Plot	558	54
Bond	Samuel		Civil War	8	85	B	
Bottesch	Andrew	B.	World War1	9	54	H	
Bowman	Walter	E.	World War1	7	40	D	
Brady	Thomas		Civil War	10	179		
Brennen	Fred	L.	Spanish American War	10	149		
Brooker	Frank	L.	World War1	12	74	B	
Brubaker	Grove	S.	Spanish American War	11	83	A	
Buckley	Hugh		Civil War	8	12	D	
Buckley	John		Civil War	6	56	A	
Buell	Charles	L.	Civil War	2	44	D	
Bullas	John	Albert	World War1	3	85	A	
Burrll	Charles	A.	Civil War	10	126	E	
Burris	Harry	A.	World War1	9	43	C	
Burton	Elijah		War of 1812	3	43	B	
Cady	George	H.	Civil War	9	33	B	
Cahoon	Reynolds		War of 1812	10	8	2	
Cain	George	R.	World War1	4	82	A	
Cairns	Charles	W.		4	45	D	
Calhoun	William	W.	Civil War	3	22 - Moved		
Callahan	Adelbert	R.	World War1	11	74	A	
Camp	Winfield	S	World War II	8	19	G	
Carey	Cornelius	(Surname may be Corey)		14	1	1	21
Carner	Frank	Wilbur	World War1	4	84	K	
Carpenter	Charles	C.	Spanish American War	11		111	

Last Name	First Name	Middle Name	War	Section	Lot	Grave	Row
Carr	Rufus	L.	World War 1	6	66	A	
Carter	Harley	Earnest	World War 1	5	4	G	
Cary	Arthur	Llewelyn	Indian War	4	54	C	
Case	Lee	Roy	World War 1	10	6	G	
Cassidy	Ralph	C.	World War 1	8	72	B	
Casterline	Frank	H.	Spanish American War	10	102	L	
Casterline	Jesse	R.	Spanish American War	10	102	B	
Casterline	Joel	P.	Civil War	10	102	J	
Chamberlain	William	H.	Civil War	13	35	J	
Chambers	Charles	Maynard	World War 1 & ll	13	41	A	
Chambers	Edwin	R.	World War 1	13	41	F	
Chapman	Alonzo		Civil War	9	58	I	
Chapman	William	H.	Civil War	13	67	I	
Clark	Edward	W.	Civil War	12	36	G	
Clark	John		Civil War	10	124	B	
Clark	Perez	G.	Civil War	12	36	J	
Clark	Richard		Civil War	11	North Plot	519	27
Coit	Henry	H.		6	17	F	
Compton	Jacob		War of 1812	6	38	A	
Conradi	John	A.	World War 1	5	12	E	
Costella	Mitchell		World War ll	9	45	L	
Cozad	Elias		War of 1812	6	1	C	
Crandall	John	E.	Civil War	5	42	J	
Crawford	Wiliam	E.	Civil War	10	82		
Crites	John		Civil War	10	Adult Graves	143	11
Crotty	Thomas	F.	Civil War	11		136	
Currier	Sargent		Civil War	2	21	D	
Dahlman	Joseph	M.	World War 1	10	31	B	
Daly	James	E.	World War 1	10	38	F	
Dart	William		Civil War	7	34	D	

171

Last Name	First Name	Middle Name	War	Section	Lot	Grave	Row
Daughtery	Charles	W.	World War 1	1	129	D	
Davis	John		Civil War	11		138	
Day	Frank	T.	World War 1	13	8	F	
Day	Joseph	A.	Civil War	12	29	G	
Derning	Dewitt	C.	Civil War	5	10	D	
Derning	Elijah	M.	Unknown	5	10	B	
DeVries	Anthony		Civil War	9	75	D	
Dewey	Eli		War of 1812	9	42	C	
DeWille	Brown		Civil War	12	55	F	
Dille	Asa		War of 1812	6	6	A	
Dille	Charles	C.	Civil War	6	6	C	
Dille	Luther		War of 1812	1	12	F	
Dille	Thomas	C.	Civil War	6	6	D	
Doan	Timothy		War of 1812	2	7	A	
Doane	John		Civil War	6	10	D	
Doane	Timothy		Revolutionary War	6	25	D	
Dodd	Herbert	L.	Spanish American War	3	97	K	
Doremus	Norton	Harold	World War 1	11	103	A	
Doughty	Thomas	D.	World War 1	13	30	F	
Draper	Arthur	Lincoln	World War 1	4	32	N	
Drukenbrod	Russell	H. Madison	World War 1	3	95	E	
Duerst	Emmanuel	Henry	World War 1	8	48	B	
Duncan	Thomas		World War ll	11	58	F	
Duty	Andrew	W.	Civil War	4	25	H	
Duty	Ebenezer		War of 1812	4	25	G	
Dyson	William	R.	Civil War	1	79	A	
Edwards	Adonijah		Revolutionary War	12	5	C	
Edwards	Rodolphus		Indian War	12	5	A	
Eggleston	Henry	P.	Civil War	11	North Plot	216	19

Last Name	First Name	Middle Name	War	Section	Lot	Grave	Row
Ehrman	George		Regular Service	10	10	K	
Ernst	Ross	E.	World War ll	10	115	F	
Farwell	Henry		Civil War	13	5	J	
Fell	Thomas		Civil War	11	63	B	
Field	William	C.	Civil War	12	33	E	
Ford	Frank	James	Civil War	2	18	H	
Ford	Hezekiah		Revolutionary War	2	41	H	
Foster	Clark	W. (Charles)	Civil War	10	52	C	
French	Edwin	C.	Civil War	10	145	A	
French	Leonard	K.	Civil War	10	183	240	
Fuller	Caleb		Civil War	4		D	
Fuller	William	Smith	Civil War	7	4	B	
Galloway	Howard	G.	Mexican War	7	72	C	
Gates	Albert	M.	Civil War	13	3	B	
Geogge	Benhardt	(Bernard)	World War l	7	66	A	
Gephart	John	S.	World War ll	13	50	F	
Gill	Ely	E.	Civil War	10	257		
Gilmore	David	S.	Civil War	6	52	Single Grave	
Givens	Edward	E.	World War l	4	91A	B	
Glassford	Albert	B.	Civil War	6	53	A	
Glenzer	Armand	(Norman)	World War ll	8	102	I	
Goad	William	Norman	World War ll	5	25	J	
Goegge	Walter	H.	World War l	9	47	3	
Gordon	John	R. (D.E.)	Spanish American War	5	50	E	
Gotts	John	(Goetz)	Civil War	10	9	F	
Gotts	John	(Goetz)	Civil War	10	9	B	
Gove	Adelbert	F.	Spanish American War	3	87		
Gray	Benjamin	J.	Civil War	13	71	496	26
Gray	James		Civil War	11	North Plot	F - Top	
Gray	Willie		Undetermined	5	84		

Last Name	First Name	Middle Name	War	Section	Lot	Grave	Row
Gray	Willie	C.	Undetermined	5	84	A	
Green	Herbert	F.	Civil War	6	4	B	
Green	William	H.	Civil War	11	90	I	
Greve	Andrew	(Andres)	Civil War	10	153		
Grigsby	William	A.	Spanish American War	9	30	G	
Grimes	Willie	D.		14		4	16
Groat	Lewis		Civil War	3	19	1	
Hadley	William	H.	Civil War	10	15	A	
Hadlock	John		Civil War	13	45	K	
Hale	Morgan		Civil War	4	49	C	
Hall	Charles	E.	Civil War	11	28	J	
Hammond	Raymond	L.		12	51	H	
Hampton	Frank	W.	World War 1	10	East Plot	447	38
Handley	John		War of 1812	2	34	C	
Hanson	Charles	(Charlie)	World War 1	10	East Plot	460	40
Hanson	Raymond	H.	U. S. Coast Guard	6	234	Single Grave	
Happel	John	F.	World War II	12	45	C	
Hararas	Christ	George	World War 1	14		2	31
Hardwick	Garry	L	Civil War	8	24	A	
Hart	Marion		Regular Service				
Hayden	Amos	S.		1	10	I	
Hendershot	Casper	A.	Spanish American War	8	19	J	
Hendershot	Hardy	M.	World War 1	8	19	D	
Hendershot	James	Abner	Civil War	8	19	L	
Hendershot	Martin	V.	Civil War	4	22		
Henderson	John	Lee		14		5	8
Henry	Roswell	C.	Civil War	7	25	A	
Hervey	William	Andrew	World War 1	10	100	D	
Hewitt	George		Civil War	12	46	E	
Higgins	Alfred	B.	Civil War	9	20	L	

Last Name	First Name	Middle Name	War	Section	Lot	Grave	Row
Higgins	Ben	F.	Civil War	9	20	E	
Higgins	Charles	N.	Civil War	9	21		
Higgins	William		War of 1812	5	11	A	36
Hill	John		Spanish American War	11	North Plot	624	
Hilliard	Albert	T.	World War 1	8	26	F	
Hink	Harry		World War 1	10	Adult Graves	271	21
Hobbs	Thomas		Civil War	10	108	I	
Hobbs	Thomas	E.	Spanish American War	10	108	C	
Holloman	Henry	W.	World War 1	8	76	B	
Hougland	Byron		Civil War	11	100		
House	James	W.	Civil War	7	1	L	
House	Ruel	H.	Civil War	7	1		
Howell	Jesse		Spanish American War	11	North Plot	228	19
Hubbell	Augustus	B.	Civil War	4	42	A	
Hudgins	Herbert		World War 1	10	Adult Graves	355	28
Hudson	Thomas	J.	Civil War	9	1	E	
Hudson	William	H.	War of 1812	9	1	D	
Hunt	James	C.	Civil War	2	59	A	
Hunter	Willie	Burl	Vietnam	2	94	C	
Hurd	Alexander		World War 1	10	88	D	
Hussong	James	H.	Civil War	4	34	D	
Hussong	Manson		Civil War	6	4	D	
Isakson	Ernest	P.	World War 1	9	13	L	
Jacobi	Henry	A.	Civil War	13	23	K	
Jacoby	John		Civil War	12			
Jayred	William	Hanson	Civil War	4	28	L	
Johnson	James		Civil War	13	64	G	
Johnson	Samuel	P.	Civil War	9	42	E	
Jones	Alva	Raymond	World War 1	2	1	C	
Jones	Edward	Hall	World War 1	10	53	E	

Last Name	First Name	Middle Name	War	Section	Lot	Grave	Row
Judson	Horace		Civil War	10	Solider Plot	1	
Juker	William	H.	Civil War	11	South Plot	177	9
Kelley	Clarence	H.	World War1	11			
Kelly	John		Civil War	1	2	A	
Kelly	John		Civil War	1	2	C	
Kent	William	H.	Civil War	10	Soldier Section 1 - (South Plot)		
Kilbourne	Austin	G.	Spanish American War	10	Walkway	842	1
Killey	Clarence	H.	World War1	11	78	L	
King	Willard	R.	World War ll	11	28	O	
Knaak	William		World War1	10	259	A	
Knudsen	Olaf	F.	World War1	2	102	D	
Konkosky	Frederick		World War1	3	57	A	
Korthals	Charles		World War1	9	119	A	
Kreager	Philip		Civil War	3	39	B	
Kuhn	Joseph	O.	World War1	10	134	E	
Lang	Frederick	J.	Civil War	11	North Plot	294	21
Lawrence	Burt	William	World War1	12	88	B	
Lawrence	William	S.	Fireman	12	67	H	
Lay	James	H.	World War1	10	179	J	
Lee	Alfred	S.	Civil War	1	16	H	
Lee	Bion		Indian War	1	16	I	
Lee	Elias		Revolutionary War	1	16		
Lester	Ezekiel		Korean War	2	36	I	
Lewis	Mozart		Spanish American War	4	64	A	
Lindsay	James	W.	Civil War	9	80	A	
Locke	Charles		Civil War	10	44	C	
Locke	Clarence	Stanley	Civil War	10	44	H	
Lockhart	William		Civil War	8	90	B	
Lovelace	Leander	M.	Civil War	10	5	L	
Lucas	William	C.	Civil War	12	35	O	

Last Name	First Name	Middle Name	War	Section	Lot	Grave	Row
Ludwig	Frank		Civil War	11	North Plot	251	19
Luster	George		Civil War	2	29	C	
Luster	Sanford	William	Civil War	8	10	F	
MacDougall	Albert	V.	World War 1	10	254	H	
Mackey	Wilson	U.	World War ll	10	149	G	
Mahaffey	Leo	James	World War 1	4	85	B	
Maisner	Charles		Civil War	13	16	I	
Maison	John	B.	Civil War	10	146	C	
Martin	Loving	Francis	World War 1	9	102	A	
Matus	Peter	Paul	World War ll	6	70	A - Top	
McIlrath	Abner	Carl	Spanish American War	10	7	K	
McIlrath	Oliver	P.	Civil War	10	7	I	
McLeod	Alex	G.	Civil War	6	44	F	
McLeod	James		Civil War	4	2	C	
McMillen	Frank		Civil War	11	22	G	
McVean	John		War of 1812	9	9	B	
Meeker	Charles	M. or W.	Civil War	2	25	E	
Meeker	Smith		War of 1812	3	35	F	
Meeker	Stephen	B.	War of 1812	7	23	G	
Miles	Manson	W. (Morison)	Civil War	12	60	C	
Miller	Daniel	P.	Civil War	12	18	K	
Miller	Emil		Civil War	13	Back of Receiving Vault - East	187	5
Miller	Frank		Civil War	12	23	J	
Miller	Harry	C.	Spanish American War	11	North Plot	450	25
Minor	Wells	C.	Civil War	5	21	B	
Moon	David	W.	World War 1	13	37	H	
Moore	Amaziah	(Amazia)	Civil War	9	70	F	
Moore	Charles	G.	World War 1	2	120	C	
Moore	John		Civil War	8	44	A	
Moore	Ralph	E.	World War ll	10	68	I	

177

Last Name	First Name	Middle Name	War	Section	Lot	Grave	Row
Morgan	Charles	R.	Spanish American War	1	2	D	
Moses	C.	Elihu	War of 1812	12	16	H	
Mott	Henry		Civil War	10	13		
Murphy	Lester	C.	World War 1	13	30	A	
Naegellen	Victor	Emmanuel	World War 1	2	71	A	
Nelson	Frank	Alexander	World War 1	11	77	L	
Nichols	Jesse		Civil War	7	37		
Norris	Henry	L.	Civil War	4	38	D	
Norton	Hazen	B.	Spanish American War	7	8	E	
Norton	James		Mexican War	7	8	M	
Norton	Walter		Civil War	7	8	C	
Norwood	Harry		World War 1	10	East Plot	504	46
Numan	Elias	G.		13	65	H	
Oldham	Edward		World War 1	3	92	J	
Oldham	Sophia	P.	World War 1	3	92	D	
Olmstead	William		Spanish American War	10	149	B	
O'Rourke	Harry	Miller	World War 1	9	17	N	
Pagett	Orville		World War 1	5	2	F	
Pahner	Albert	B.	World War 1	2	114	B	
Papworth	Robert	Reed	Civil War	11	26	M	
Parks	Samuel		Civil War	5	7		
Parks	William		World War 1	6	384	Single Grave	
Pfaff	George		Civil War	10	Adult Graves	91	7
Pickett	William	H.	Civil War	11	South Plot	42	2
Piggott	Percy	W.	World War 1	10	103	I	
Piper	William	Wirt	Civil War	3	83	B	
Poak	Lycurgus	A.	Civil War	5	28	Single Grave	
Poland	Norman	B.	World War 1	2	97	D	
Pope	Byron		Civil War	9	9	J	
Pratt	Isaac	H.	Civil War	7	33	D	

Last Name	First Name	Middle Name	War	Section	Lot	Grave	Row
Prince	Lloyd	A.	World War1	5	98	B	
Quilliams	William	Thomas	Civil War	10	67	J	
Radtke	Ellwood	Lee	World War1	4	74	F	
Rand	Benjamin	F.	Civil War	9	56	K	
Randall	Joseph	Ted	World War1	4	71	F	
Rash	William	Arthur	Spanish American War	13	59	F	
Rauch	Louis	John	World War1	3	45	D	
Reader	Charles	E.	Civil War	9	48	B	
Reader	Charles	Marshall	Spanish American War	9	48	E	
Reading	George	S.	Civil War	3	25	J	
Reed	Franklin	T.	Civil War	10	43	J	
Reed	Robert		World War1	10	270	D	
Reeder	Schrole		Spanish American War	2	51	C	
Reese	David		World War1	10	North Plot	788	89
Rehr	William	F.	Civil War	11	North Plot	89	13
Richards	John	Gooding	Civil War	2	33	A	
Richardson	Joseph	B.	Civil War	6	55		
Richmond	Thomas	C.	Civil War	3	18	A	
Ridgeway	Roy			14		2	21
Roberts	Charles	O.	Civil War	3	14	F	
Robinson	Frank	A.	Spanish American War	6	390	C	
Romanis	Harold		World War1	4	74	A	
Rooney	James		World War1	11	North Plot	435	25
Ruple	Charles		Civil War	10	137	A	
Moon	David	W.	world War I	13	57	H	
Moore	Amaziah	(Amazia)	Civil War	9	70	F	
Moore	Charles	G.	World War1	2	120	C	
Moore	John		Civil War	8	44	A	
Moore	Ralph	E.	World WarII	10	68	I	
Scata	Sebastiano		World WarII	6	54	P	

Last Name	First Name	Middle Name	War	Section	Lot	Grave	Row
Schlegel	Benjamin	F.	Regular Service	11	66	E	
Schneider	Karl		Civil War	1	52	A	
Schuster	John	J.	Civil War	4	12	E	
Scott	Edward	G.	World War I	10	250	H	
Scott	George	W.	Civil War	5	10	K	
Scott	George	A.	World War I	10	North Plot	643	67
Scott	John	W.	Spanish American War	13	67	E	
Scott	Lawrence	C.	Civil War	6		404	
Seab	Cornell	T.	World War II	14		3	22
Seaberg	Carl		World War I	3	95	L	
Seaman	Emil	Henry	World War II	11			
Sepe	Carmen		World War I	10	North Plot	812	94
Sequin	Charles		World War I	10	Adult Graves	313 - 1/2	24
Severance	Malvern	W.	World War I	3	22	E	
Severance	Robert	E.	World War II	3	22	F	
Sharp	Irvie	D.	World War I	4	48	D	
Shay	Henry	B.	Civil War	9	7	A	
Sheen	James		World War I	11	North Plot	241	19
Shepard	Lorin		Civil War	10	20	H	
Sherman	Albert	S.	Civil War	9	10	A	
Sherman	Clark (Charles)	J. (Shennan)	Spanish American War	11	North Plot	308	21
Sherman	Harry	Merle	World War I	5	25	H	
Sherman	William	A.	Civil War	9	49	C	
Siebert	Elroy			10	North Plot	714 - 1/2 - Top	77
Silsby	Alonzo		Civil War	3	33	C	
Silsby	Sylvester	S.	Civil War	13	59	K	
Simmons	William	W.	World War I	12	83, 84 & 89-116	101	
Simpson	William	H.	Spanish American War	6	227	Single Grave	
Sinnott	John		Civil War	4	24	C	
Sisco	Kenneth	L.		11	22	L	

Last Name	First Name	Middle Name	War	Section	Lot	Grave	Row
Six	Walter	Pannett	World War II	10	117	B	
Slaght	Cornelius		Civil War	3	21	G	
Smith	James		Civil War	4	22	B	
Smith	James	D.	Spanish American War	9	7	H	
Smith	Nathan		Civil War	10		622	
Smith	Robert	W.	World War II	5	106		
Snyder	Mary	E.	Civil War	11	91	Single Grave	
Soule	Nathan		Civil War	9	22	A	
Soule	Theron	C.	Civil War	9	22	I	
Speidel	Richard		World War I	3	3	E	
Spielhaupter	Martin	C.	Unknown	7	39	J	
Stafford	George	W.	Civil War	12	41	C	
Stafford	Orlando		Civil War	6	29	H	
Stark	James		Civil War	12	3	D	
Stark	Lewis	D. (Louis)	Civil War	9	61	E	
Starkweather	Jacob		Civil War	13	150		1
Steinfurt	Louis	C.	World War I	1	Back of Receiving Vault - East	C	
Stokes	Harry	M.	Civil War	11	120	D	
Strong	George	D.	Civil War	1	63	A	
Strong	John	W.	Spanish American War	1	21	L	
Swain	Alexander		Civil War	11	21		
Tait	Clifford	R.	World War I	10	North Plot	402	24
Taylor	Buel	G.	Civil War	10	Adult Graves	215	17
Telling	James		Civil War	11	54		
Thomas	Frank	M.	Civil War	6	96	H	
Thomas	William	M.	Civil War	4	33	B	
Thompson	John		World War I	2	19	D	
Thompson	Thomas		Unknown	10	162	Single Grave	
Thompson	William		Civil War	4	120		
Thorp	Frank	W.	Civil War	12	57	C	
					12	A	

Last Name	First Name	Middle Name	War	Section	Lot	Grave	Row
Tillitzke	Walter	C.	World War1	6	93	Single Grave	
Todd	Carl	Stewart	World War1	5	78	C	
Todd	Joseph	N.	World War1	6		482	
Trusty	William	E.	World War1	13	Back of Receiving Vault - East	186	5
Tucker	Claude	Edward	Spanish American War	10	108	D	
Tuttle	Jerome		Civil War	9	22	F	
Tyler	Daniel	S.	War of 1812	8	36	G	
Tyler	George	E.	Civil War	8	36		
Uterhark	Walter	F.	World War1	10	23	K	
Valentine	George		Civil War	11		129	
Vance	A.	Max	Spanish American War	11	North Plot	164	17
Voelker	Max		World War1	11	North Plot	240	19
Wallace	George		Unknown	10	Adult Graves	408	33
Walworth	Warren	F.	Civil War	2	26	E	
Wells	John	R.	Civil War	12	83, 84 & 89-116	48	
West	Elmer	A.	Civil War	1	2	F	
Wetzel	Peter		Civil War	10	Soliders Plat 2		
Whaley	Lucius	D.	Civil War	4	11	F	
Wheeler	John	H.	Civil War	11		37 or 87	
Wheeler	William	H.	Civil War	11	16	F	
Wilcox	Edwin	E.	Civil War	11	10		
Wilhelm	John		World War1	5	144	Single Grave	
Williams	Ortan		Civil War	11		143	
Wills	Russell		World War ll	9	56	C	
Willson	Charles	B.	Civil War	6	52	C	
Willson	Frederick		National Guard	6	52	M	
Willson	Frederick	J.		6	52	R	
Willson	George	A.	Civil War	6	52	E	
Willson	James	P.	Civil War	6	52	D	
Wilson	Arthur	Shepard	World War 1	5	77	E	

Last Name	First Name	Middle Name	War	Section	Lot	Grave	Row
Wilson	Arthur	S.	World War 1	10	19	I	
Wilson	Samuel	G.	Undetermined	10	185	B	
Wilson	Vernon	W.	World War 1	8	112	B	
Wilson	William	David		14		3	26
Wolf	Frederick		Civil War	2	66	B	
Woniack	Edward		World War 1	11	Old West Plot	314	18
Wood	Arthur	R.	Spanish American War	11	North Plot	586	31
Wood	James	L.	Spanish American War	11	South Plot	106	5
Woodworth	Luther	E.	Civil War	13	18	K	
Yannetta	Alexandro		World War 1	10	Adult Graves	156 - 1/2	12
Yea	Kenneth	D.	World War ll	9	74	L	
Zackosky	Harry	E.	Regular Service	11	57	E	

Table 8: Victims of the Collinwood School Fire

Last Name	First Name	Middle Name	Section	Lot	Grave	Row
Bravo	Floy	I.	10	192	F	
Burrows	Amelia	Hazel	11	South Plot	29	2
Centner	Lester		11	North Plot	47	8
Day	Percy		12	30	F	
Ewald	Florence		10	94	C	
Grushauge	Mary		10	Baby Graves	25	2
Hummel	Esther		11	North Plot	44	7
Kanowski	Edward		11	67	A	
Meirt	Eddie	(Edward)	10	Baby Graves	24	2
Puffel	Gretchen		10	94		
Sheppard	Morris	C.	11	99	F	

Last Name	First Name	Middle Name	Section	Lot	Grave	Row
Sprung	Alvin		10	94	H	
Smith	Willie		11	67	E	
Walden	Lulu		12	25	L	
Wachhaus	Eva		11	67	D	
Wachhaus	Ida		11	67	D	

Bibliography

Annals of the Early Settlers Association of Cuyahoga County

Bellamy, John Stark (III). *They Died Crawling and Other Tales of Cleveland Woe* (Gray & Company, Publishers, 1995).

Cigliano, Jan. *Showplace of America, Cleveland's Euclid Avenue, 1850-1910* (Kent State University Press, Kent, Ohio, 1991).

Cleveland Congregationalists 1895, Historical Sketches of our Twenty-five Churches and Missions and their Work in Missions-Local Grown and Social Life with Full Directories of Members to January 1, 1896. Edited by Rev. A. B. Cristy, Pastor Lake View Congregational Church. (The Williams Publishing and Electric Co. 1896).

Cleveland Herald

Cleveland Leader

Cleveland Plain Dealer.

Cleveland Press.

Etlin, Richard A. The *Architecture of Death, The Transformation of the Cemetery in Eighteenth-Century Paris* (The MIT Press, Cambridge, Massachusetts and London, England, 1987).

Galbreath, Charles B. *History of Ohio* (The American Historical Society, Inc, Chicago and New York, 1928).

Hayden, A. S. *Early History of The Disciples in the Western Reserve, Ohio.* (Chase & Hall Publishers, 1876).

Howe, Henry. *Historical Collections of Ohio* (State of Ohio, The Laning Printing Co., Public Printers, Norwalk, Ohio, 1888).

Jackson, Kenneth T. and Vergara, Camilo Jose. *Silent Cities, The Evolution of the American Cemetery* (Princeton Architectural Press, New York, New York, 1989).

Johnson, Crisfield. *History of Cuyahoga County, Ohio* (D.W. Ensign & Co., 1879).

Kennedy, James Harrison. *A History of The City of Cleveland, Its Settlement, Rise and Progress, 1796-1896.* The Imperial Press, Cleveland, 1896.

Larick, Roy and Semsel, Craig. *Euclid Township, 1796-1801, Protest in the Western Reserve* (Western Reserve Historical Society and Euclid Historical Society, 2003).

Memorial Record of the County of Cuyahoga and City of Cleveland Ohio (The Lewis Publishing Company, 1894).

Post, Charles Asa. *Doans Corners and the City Four Miles West* (The Caxton Company, 1930).

Price, Ellen Loughry. *A History of East Cleveland (1970).*

Rice, Harvey. *Pioneers of The Western Reserve* (Lee and Shepard Publisher, Boston; Charles T. Dillingham, New York 1883).

Rice, Harvey. *Sketches of Western Reserve Life* (William W. Williamson, Cleveland OH, 1885).

Rose, William Ganson. *Cleveland The Making of a City* (The World Publishing Company 1950).

Rose, Mrs. W.G., Chairman. *Album of the Western Reserve Centennial. Published under the auspices of the Woman's Department* . (Edwin H. Clark & Co., Publishers, 1896).000000000000000

Sloane, David Charles. *The Last Great Necessity, Cemeteries in American History* (The Johns Hopkins University Press, Baltimore, MD and London, England, 1991).

Tarlow, Sarah. *Landscapes of Memory: The Nineteenth-Century Garden Cemetery* (Europoean Journal of Archaeology Vol. 3(2):217-239).

Village Green to City Center, 1843-1943, Centennial of The Euclid Avenue Congregational Church, Cleveland, Ohio (Artcraft Printing Company, Cleveland, Ohio 1943).

Whittlesey, Col. Charles. *Early History of Cleveland, Ohio* (Fairbanks Benedict & Co. Printers, Herald Office Cleveland, 1867

Wickham, Gertrude Van Rensselaer. *The Pioneer Families of Cleveland, 1796 – 1840* (The Executive Committee of the Woman's Department of the Cleveland Centennial Commission-1896. Evangelical Publishing House, 1914).

Endnotes

1 Cleveland Plain Dealer, "Forebears lie in tract of shame", Brent Larkin, July 3, 1988.

2 *Annals of the Early Settlers Association of Cuyahoga County*, 1916.

3 Wickham, Gertrude Van Rensselaer, *The Pioneer Families of Cleveland*, Evangelical Publishing House, 1914, Page 138.

4 Euclid Avenue Congregational Church, Manuscript 3577, Container 14, Western Reserve Historical Society.

5 Euclid Avenue Congregational Church, Manuscript 3577, Container 14, Western Reserve Historical Society.

6 Edward F. Grose, *Centennial History of the Village of Ballston Spa*, The Ballston Journal, 1907, Page 26.

7 *Annals of the Early Settlers' Association of Cuyahoga County*, 1896; Pgs. 661 to 662.

8 William Ganson Rose, *Cleveland, The Making of a City*, The World Publishing Company, 1950, page 64.

9 Euclid Avenue Congregational Church, Manuscript 3577, Container 14, Western Reserve Historical Society.

10 S. J. Kelly, "The Story of An Old Church", *Cleveland Plain Dealer*, December 9, 1943.

11 Charles Asa Post, *Doan's Corners and the City Four Miles West*, The Caxton Company, 1930, page 61.

12 *George Watkins, Trustees of the Burying Ground Association in the East part of Cleveland near what is known as Doan's Corners v. The Euclid Avenue Congregational Church*, Cuyahoga County Common Pleas Case Numbers 48218 and 48219. Case number 48218 was dismissed by the Plaintiff on April 21, 1896 at his costs, with case number 48219 remaining.

13 *George Watkins, Trustees of the Burying Ground Association in the East part of Cleveland near what is known as Doan's Corners v. The Euclid Avenue Congregational Church*, Cuyahoga County Circuit Court Case Number 1685, Cuyahoga County Archives.

14 Euclid Avenue Congregational Church, Manuscript 3577, Container 14, Western Reserve Historical Society.

15 *George Watkins, Trustees of the Burying Ground Association in the East part of Cleveland near what is known as Doan's Corners v. The Euclid Avenue Congregational Church*, Cuyahoga County Circuit Case Number 1685, Judge Burrows' final decision, Cuyahoga County Archives.

16 *The Cleveland Leader*, "Quit Claim Donations. Secret Committee of the G.A.R. Is After Them," June 11, 1901.

17 *Cleveland Plain Dealer*, "Old Cemetery Property", January 9, 1898.

18 *The Cleveland Press*, "Tavern Keeper Lost Loved Ones Within Three Years. Mother, Father, Wife and Daughter All Died–He was Buried Beside Them Seven Years Later–Mute Testimony of Time-Worn Stones," April 6, 1904.

19 Charles Asa Post, *Doan's Corners and the City Four Miles West,* The Caxton Company, 1930, pages 89 and 90.

20 *Village Green to City Center; 1843-1943, page 67.*

21 S.J. Kelly, "An Old Church Passes," *Cleveland Plain Dealer*, December 24, 1943.

22 Odell Cozad Abstracting Company Records, Manuscript 4598, Western Reserve Historical Society.

[23]   A standard Gunter chain consisted of 100 iron links of equal length, and measured 66 feet. Each link in the chain measured 7.92 inches. The first and last links are handles. Every ten links there is a brass tag that identifies the number of links. At link 10 and link 90, the tag has one point. At link 20 and link 80, the tag has two points. At 30 and 70, three points, and at 40 and 60, four points. At link 50, the halfway point, a round tag is used. It is assumed that this was the type of chain utilized to measure this lot. For example, in the deed where it indicates 5 chains and 3 links to stone, the measurements could be calculated into feet and inches as follows:

5 chains * 66 feet = 330 feet

3 links * 7.92 inches = 23.76 inches or 1 foot 11.76 inches

During this period of time feet and inches were not utilized when surveying property. A reference to a stone was in fact a stone located at a point on the property. A picture of the Gunter chain is shown below:

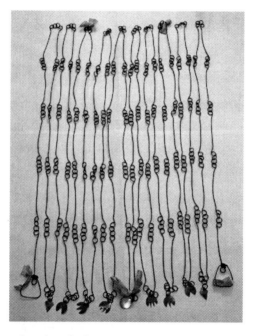

Produced and Photographed by David Manthey
http://www.orbitals.com/

[24] Price, Ellen Loughry; *A History of East Cleveland*; 1970.

[25] Cleveland Plain Dealer, "East Cleveland-A Name Often Used", S.J. Kelly; April 9, 1940.

[26] An Inventory of Special Governmental Agencies in Cuyahoga County; Governmental Research Institute; January, 1976.

[27] Cleveland Plain Dealer, "The Fifth East Cleveland", S. J. Kelly; July 3, 1940.

[28] Showplace of America, Cleveland's Euclid Avenue 1850-1910; Jan Cigliano; The Kent State University Press; 1991.

[29] Cleveland Press, "Three Suburbs Claim Cemetery"; March 26, 1930.

[30] Cleveland Heights, City Managers Files, Manuscript LR-MUN-0091, Western Reserve Historical Society.

[31] Cleveland Press, "City's 'Orphan Cemetery Prospers Without Owner", July 6, 1938.

[32] Cleveland Plain Dealer, "E. Cleveland Foster Mom to Cemetery", March 1960.

[33] Call and Post, "Who's Minding the East-Cleveland-Cleveland Heights Cemetery?", Armetta Landrum, October 20, 1994.

[34] Cleveland Plain Dealer, "Cemetery ailing", Evelyn Theiss, October 27, 1998.

[35] Ancestry.com. *Connecticut Marriages to 1800* [database online]. Orem, UT: MyFamily.com, Inc., 1997. Original data: Bailey, Frederic W. *Early Connecticut Marriages as Found on Ancient Church Records prior to 1800*. New Haven, CT: Bureau of American Ancestry, 1896-1906.

[36] Zebina Moses, Historical sketches of John Moses of Plymouth, a settler of 1632 to 1640: John Moses of Windsor and Simsbury, a settler prior to 1647; and John Moses, of Portsmouth, a settler prior

to 1640: also a genealogical record of some of their descendants, Press of the Case, Lockwood & Brainard Co., 1890-1907.

37 Ohio State History of the Daughters of the American Revolution, Molly Chittenden Chapter, Geauga County, Ohio, page 492-493.

38 *Cleveland Plain Dealer*, Death's Flames, An Early Evening Fire and Its Disastrous Results, November 16, 1891.

39 *Cleveland Plain Dealer*, Search for the Dead. Fireman Work to Recover Capt. Grady's Body", November 17, 1891.

40 *Cleveland Plain Dealer*," Grady in His Grave", November 21, 1891.

41 *Cleveland Press*, "Captain John Grady", November 16, 1891

42 John Stark Bellamy, *They Died Crawling and Other Tales of Cleveland Wow*, Gray & Company Publishers, Cleveland; 1995; pages 144-146.

43 *Cleveland Press*, March 4, 1908, page 4.

44 *Annals Early Settlers Association of Cuyahoga County*, 1931, pages 9 and 10.

45 *Annals of the Early Settlers Association of Cuyahoga County*, 1882, pages 65 and 66.

46 *History of Bennington County, VT with Illustrations and Biographical Sketches of Some of Its Prominent Men and Pioneers*, D. Mason & Co., Publishers; Syracuse, N.Y., 1889, pages 363 and 364.

47 Gertrude Van Rensselaer Wickham, *The Pioneer Families of Cleveland*, Evangelical Publishing House, 1914, pages 255 and 256.

48 S.J. Kelly, "They Practiced Medicine for Near a Century", *Cleveland Plain Dealer*, October 21, 1940.

49 *Annals of the Early Settlers Association of Cuyahoga County*, 1931, pages 31 and 32.

50 *Annals of the Early Settlers Association of Cuyahoga County*, 1890, pages 425-427.

51 *The Official Roster of the Soldiers of the American Revolution Buried in the State of Ohio*, 1990, page 106. *Official Roster lll, Soldiers of the American Revolution Who Lived in the State of Ohio*, 1959, page 435.

52 Gertrude Van Rensselaer Wickham, *Pioneer Families of Cleveland, 1796-1840*, Evangelical Publishing House, 1914, page 69.

53 William R. Coates, *A history of Cuyahoga County and the city of Cleveland*, American Historical Society, 1924, page 250.

54 William R. Coates, *A history of Cuyahoga County and the city of Cleveland*, American Historical Society, 1924, page 444.

55 *Roster of Ohio Soldiers in the War of 1812; The Adjutant General of Ohio*, 1916, page 93.

56 A.S. Hayden, *Early History of The Disciples in the Western Reserve, Ohio*, Chase & Hall Publishers, 1875, pages 408 and 415.

57 William R. Coates, *A history of Cuyahoga County and the city of Cleveland*, American Historical Society, 1924, page 284.

58 *Annals of the Early Settlers Association of Cuyahoga County*, 1881, pages 65-68.

59 Massachusetts Soldiers and Sailors, page 804.

60 Henry M. Selden, *Haddam Neck, History of Middlesex County*, J.B. Beers, publisher, New York, 1884.

61 Allene Beaumont Duty, *Duty Family, The Descendants of Ebenezer Duty of Ohio*, Cleveland, Ohio 1972.

62 Henry Howe, LL.D., *Historical Collections of Ohio*, The Lansing Printing Co., Norwalk, OH, 1898, pages 642-643.

63 Wilfred Henry Alburn and Miriam Russell Alburn, *This Cleveland of Our;* The S. J. Clarke Publishing Company, 1933. Harriet Taylor

Upton, *History of the Western Reserve,* Lewis Publishing Company, 1991.

[64] *The Cleveland Leader,* "Forty Years a Street Railway Superintendent in Cleveland", September 16, 1900.

[65] Rudolphus Edwards papers, 1794-1869 (1794-1818), Western Reserve Historical Society, MS.466.

[66] *Annals of the Early Settlers Association of Cuyahoga County,* 1883, pages 47-48.

[67] S. J. Kelly, "Rodolphus Edwards – Cleveland's Unofficial Mayor", *Cleveland Plain Dealer,* February 7, 1939.

[68] *Annals of the Early Settlers Association of Cuyahoga County,* pages 465-466.

[69] Elbert Jay Benton, *Cultural Story of An American City, Cleveland,* Western Reserve Historical Society, 1943, page 43.

[70] Gertrude Van Rensselaer Wickham, *The Pioneer Families of Cleveland, 1796-1840,* Evangelical Publishing House, 1914, pages 618-619.

[71] *Cleveland Plain Dealer,* "Glance at the History of Cleveland", September 7, 1859.

[72] Ancestry.com. *History of North Central Ohio.* Provo, UT. MyFamily. com, Inc. 2004. History of North Central Ohio: embracing Richland, Ashland, Wayne, Medina, Lorain, Huron and Knox Counties. Duff, William A. Topeka. Historical Pub. Co.. 1991. Page 74

[73] *Annals of the Early Settlers Association of Cuyahoga County,* 1881, pages 53-54.

[74] *History of Macomb County, Michigan.* M.A. Leeson & Co., 1882.

[75] *Massachusetts Soldiers & Sailors of the Revolutionary War.* Wright & Potter Printing Co., 1902, pages 631 and 632.

[76] *Cleveland Herald,* February 2, 1832.

77   William R. Coates, *A History of Cuyahoga County and the City of Cleveland*, American Historical Society, 1924, Page 1_474.

78   *Annals of the Early Settlers Association of Cuyahoga County*, 1882, page 41.

79   *Memorial Record of the County of Cuyahoga and City of Cleveland, Ohio;* Chicago: The Lewis Publishing Company; 1894; page 198.

80   *Annals of the Early Settlers Association of Cuyahoga County*, 1883, page 38.

81   *Annals of the Early Settlers Association of Cuyahoga County*, 1911, page 78.

82   *Annals of the Early Settlers Association of Cuyahoga County*, 1885, pages 59-69.

83   S. J. Kelly, "Watkins of Watkins Glen", *Cleveland Plain Dealer*, May 21, 1946.

84   S. J. Kelly, "The Name of Watkins Glen", *Cleveland Plain Dealer*, May 29, 1946.

85   *Annals of the Early Settlers Association of Cuyahoga County*, 1887, pages 155-156.

About the Author

Nancy Fogel West was born in 1957 in Berea, Ohio the daughter of Richard F. and Arlene M. (nee Gutzman) Fogel, she has one son Bryan C. West. Ms. West graduated from Baldwin Wallace College in 1993 with a BA in Business Administration. In her professional career Ms. West provides consulting and customer service to employers in connection with their workers' compensation and safety programs.

Ms. West currently holds the position of Vice President and Assistant Secretary of the East Cleveland Township Cemetery Foundation and continues to work to renovate and revitalize this cemetery.

Printed in the United States
80495LV00003B/172-237